SELLING:
Powerful New Strategies for Sales Success

18 Secret Strategies and Hundreds of Fresh Insights for Success in Selling Make This Book the Most Important on Selling Since Jeffrey Gitomer's Sales Bible

SELLING:
Powerful New Strategies for Sales Success

Kevin Hogan Psy.D. • Dave Lakhani
Gary May • Eliot Hoppe
Larry Kevin Adams • Mollie Marti Ph.D.

Network 3000 Publishing
3432 Denmark Ave. #108
Eagan, MN 55123

Selling: Powerful New Strategies for Sales Success

Library of Congress Cataloging-in-Publication Data
Hogan, Kevin
Selling: Powerful New Strategies for Sales Success/
by Kevin Hogan, Dave Lakhani, Mollie Marti, Gary May,
Larry Adams, Eliot Hoppe

Includes Bibliographic references and index.
1. Selling 2. Sales
HF 5438.25.H62   2008
658.85-dc22   2008

ISBN: 1-934266-04-3
ISBN: 978-1-934266-04-5
Hardcover

Printed in the United States of America
Published by
Network 3000 Publishing
(612) 616-0732
www.network3000publishing.com

This book is available in quantity discounts.
For more information, call (US) 612-616-0732.

CONTENTS

An Introduction That's Worth Reading...

The Selling No One Understands

Without you, no one else has a job.

The salesperson doesn't make a sale? There is no money to pay the janitor, the CEO, the customer service rep, the IT people, the graphics gal, the advertising guy.

You should see the faces of the people who actually don't generate money in company when I make that statement.

In 2 seconds I can scan an audience and tell who is who. Of course it isn't rocket science to distinguish real smiles of appreciation and plastic pasted on faces.

But the facts are the facts. The people who aren't bringing in money are what are known as "expenses" or "liabilities." The people who bring money into the business are known as "assets."

Yet, no one says, "I want to be a salesperson when I grow up."

And it ticks me off.

In the United States, on average salespeople earn far more than almost all other professions.

The selling profession gets no respect from the ignorant.

I've been selling since I was 9 years old. I had to. We grew up poor in Chicago. Really poor. The choices were minimal. I sold to survive. I sold greeting cards. I sold my body to pick weeds, shovel driveways of snow, cut the grass for people...and over the next 35 years I sold what seems to be just about everything.

And rarely was I afforded respect for selling.

Let me tell you point blank:

Without you, no on in your company eats.

Without you, no one in your family eats.

Without you, your country goes bankrupt.

You aren't the only one that matters, but you matter far more than any other person in your company.

The Sales Manager or V.P. that bought you this book gets that.

If you beat them to it, maybe it makes sense that you give them a copy of this book, as it will make them better at what they do.

The Sales Team that authored this book is one of the most successful and diverse groups of people you could hope for.

And I have a confession...

...I asked each author to share their best material in their specific selling niche. The information you are about to drink in is flat out mind blowing.

7

"Objections," which have paralyzed you for decades are blasted away. Presentations are made easy and motivation is made permanent. If this isn't the finest book on selling ever written, it's in the top handful.

You won't find hype in this book. You'll find out how to go from selling well to being a star. You'll find out how to go from being a star to being a superstar in selling. Everyone here has caused the wheels of the world to turn.

They say love makes the world go 'round. It doesn't. Salespeople do.

What I like about selling is that it requires all the skills, talents and integrity that it takes to never wonder or worry where the next dollar comes from.

I had an email from one of the people in my Inner Circle the other day. If you wish, you can find out information about the Inner Circle here: http://www.kevinhogan.com/innercircle.htm

It was a very simple question. Here's what she asked: "What do I do when I don't get paid what my male counterparts are getting paid?"

My answer, "Leave."

If the person had been selling for their company instead of sitting in an office, they'd have a chance to show what they were made of. But that isn't the case. This person wanted something "given" to them that they "deserved."

In selling, there is no "deserve" and nothing is ever "given" to the salesperson.

The salesperson doesn't get to have a salary that is protected by a bunch of laws created by government bureaucrats that have maybe "sold out," but don't generate income.

The salesperson has to work with the highest level of integrity, force of personality, love for people, caring for his company and her family.

No one else in the company has to work all 8 hours in a day. They slack off, surf the Internet and dink around at the water cooler while the salesperson is out busting her butt paying for everyone to do that.

And there are no exceptions to this.

Either someone is bringing in revenue for the company, or they are spending the revenue you generate.

Period.

Do you have my respect?

You better believe it.

You have more than that. You have my appreciation.

Salespeople are the only force that causes society to exist.

When you break it down to kindergarten terms, the reason a government can tax is because you generated all the money for everyone to take home.

Are you all that matters?

No.

(Sorry.)

The rest of the world matters, too. Other people play important roles in the world. Respect what they do. Simply realize that you make the world go 'round...K.H.

What's In This Book for You?

When you assemble a professional sports team, you get everything from electric personalities to the guys with work ethics that can't be stopped. Hopefully you get as many stars as you can to win the Super Bowl. That's what I did with this book.

Bringing together six people to create a book for you that would be like no other book on selling you've read.

Our first objective is to show you something new. I hate buying something and getting what I got in someone else's book. When I write a book I like to write fresh material and offer secrets that haven't previously been let out of the bag. You'll find lots of distinctions in this book that you might have wondered about but now know the answer.

You'll be inspired by this book. You'll take action because of this book. This book will show you new skills and strategies you would never have thought of prior to reading it.

And because this is a team of salespeople writing for you, you're going to want to learn more about those people that resonate most with you. Biographies are at the back of the book along with website and contact information. Write them and thank them for giving what they have given. I asked for a lot from this team and they came through.

We have authors from four continents. That means you will be unfamiliar with some styles of writing. That's OK. That's part of what makes you great. Adapting to the diverse is a key trait of successful salespeople. Don't let unusual spellings of a word ("realize" in the USA is "realise" in the UK) throw you.

Each author wrote with the required outcome of giving you something that would help you get away from being "good" and move you toward being a superstar.

What you won't find is what is in all the other books about selling out there. This is not a step-by-step guide. It is a well-designed collection of gifts from each salesperson to you. Obviously there is a structure to it, but each chapter is a complete experience on its own. I like to think of it as a round table of superstars that answer questions about motivation, passion, strategy, techniques, tactics, closing, long-term relationships and everything else that matters.

I've written extensively on selling in other books. If you want a step-by-step guide pick up one of those books. This book is not a step-by-step guide. This book is for you! You are the person who wants to learn something new and often powerful and profound.

Finally, all of my co-authors here are probably better writers than I am; yet I'll be popping in occasionally with *[Ed. Notes]*

Sometimes you'll want to know something about who is writing and they were too humble to tell you. Sometimes I'll simply not be able to help myself in wielding this new power that I have. (I've never been the editor before, so I want to get everything I can out of this experience.)

For me life is serious.

John Lennon said, "This ain't no dress rehearsal."

But life is also meant to be fun and although it is not my intent to change anyone's writing style, *I retained the right to HAVE FUN in this book with you and my fellow authors in my occasional editorial notes!*

You've already been through Sales 101.

Now you meet the Pros. The questions have already been asked...now you get the answers.

PART ONE:
THE OUTER GAME OF SELLING

Chapter One

Buying Back The Sale?!

[Ed. Note- Gary May is from the U.K. and one of the finest sales trainers I've met. Gary's approach to selling is awesome and it's why he's in the top 1%. When he spoke at my event, Influence: Boot Camp 2007, he had the audience absolutely riveted. I asked Gary to pen the first section of the book. And forgive the English for the English learned to spell "learned," as learnt. I assure you we remain faithful to the U.K. reader and remind American readers that there are more than one or two ways to spell the same word... depending on what country you are in!]

So there you are, you have sat in front of a customer for the past two hours, and your presentation is going really well until the customer stops you in mid-flow and says, "Thanks for coming in today, Gary, it has been a revelation to hear about your product and how it will integrate with our company's plan and ethos. How much is it going to cost?"

Gary: "OK, that will be $350,000."

Customer: "That's great. How would you like that, by electronic bank transfer or would you prefer cash?"

This, I imagine, is how many, if not all of your sales presentations end up with zero closing, zero objections, no haggling on price and the customer holding his pen ready to sign.

What do you mean, "IF ONLY!"

Well to be honest, I have hardly ever come across such a straightforward sale either, and if that had been my experience, I don't think I would have enjoyed sales as much as I do. However, does 'selling' have to be as difficult as some books, websites, trainers, managers and we make it?

Today, I want to make what we do as easy and as straight forward as possible because I have never been totally convinced by previous material which concludes the sale with a solution to a "tricky" objection or a "clever close". This is partly due to the fact that a number of my presentations have ended with the customer saying, "Nice 'close', Gary, what else have you got?"

The problem is that these techniques have been around for some thirty years now and you have to consider a little but often ignored point: In the main, customers ARE professional non-buyers!

Now, I'm sorry if this upsets you but I have a couple of points for you to read and consider:

1: Customers DO understand that a discount for today WILL apply tomorrow no matter how strongly you tell them otherwise.

2: A discount due to a "cancellation" of someone else's order is not only fantastic timing but is often complete fabrication.

3: Most CEO's will know, maybe not by name but in practice what a "Benjamin Franklin" or "Churchill" close is.

4: "You need to ACT NOW as this is my last one and we won't be getting another for at least a month" means: YOU HAVE NO BUSINESS for the next month as your job is to sell this product which you claim you don't have. I can't believe salespeople still use this!

There you go, four examples where a customer knows more about sales than the sales person because they have not kept up with the latest techniques and still rely on methods that are a century old!

Key Point: Customers and clients are professional non-buyers and know exactly what works in getting you out the door WITHOUT a decision.

So where do you look for the latest USABLE techniques and strategies? Personally I have never really found it practical, in the heat of the moment, to look out for where a customer's eyes are looking, listening to hear whether he is using auditory or kinesthetic language patterns or trying to pace my breathing with their breathing. All of these methods I am sure have their place within the arena of influence but for me, having one, to one and half hours with a client made it far too complicated and often clouded what I was trying to do. **My sole outcome is, to get the customer to see my product, service or idea as a must have for his business and its future prosperity.**

This then is the basis for what we are going to be doing in this chapter. You will discover some new and recently proven methods of getting the customer orclient to see himself and his company using your products and services in such a way that to, "say NO" will actually do him, his company and staff an injustice.

Names DO Matter More Than Most Anyone Would Guess

To start with I would like to concentrate on the power of somebody's name.

As you will find out in the upcoming chapter on Role Projection, a name can carry a whole character, set of values and can often determine how you feel about a person before you actually meet with them. Additionally a name attached to someone you already know is just as powerful, as this too has encoded within it many preconceptions of them, your previous experiences with them, how you feel about them and will cause you to display a physical response. Think about a friend you have who is known for their brilliant sense of humor. What happens when their name comes up in conversation? The chances are that simply mentioning that person's name will create a smile on your face showing physically how you feel about them. How useful could that one piece of information be to you?

Whose names will your customer react to?

To answer this I have to ask you another question. If you were to present a product or service to a CEO but related the benefits towards a staff member he liked or respected and showing him how happy they would be, would this cause internal conflict if he were to say no to your offer?

Put another way. "I bet your kids would be so happy, love you forever and think you were the best Dad ever if you bought home this games station for them, wouldn't they?" If you are a parent you will know exactly how this statement causes all sorts of internal conflict in the decision making process because you either experience the pain of guilt when you see your kids or you buy the product.

This will be addressed a little later.

Who Works For Whom?

Do you work for your company or do they work for you? The answer could be either one in most peoples' mind. Can I suggest to you who is really the boss and who has the control?

Why do people start their own business?

Generally people who start their own company have a desire to be in control of their own destiny, have a need to make their own money and not be completely in the hands of someone else, and want to provide comfort and security to those who they love and feel they have made a difference to their families' and employees' lives.

So how are you going to be utilizing their need for security and the need to please others in your sales presentations?

I want to you to think about whom the customer is providing security for and whom is he trying to please. The immediate answer is his family as it is they that benefit from the proceeds of his company, but isn't it also true that he would want job security for, and gratitude from, the people who work for him?

If looked at in a slightly different way that means that THEY (the staff) become his 'work family' and it is for them that he is working. Lets face it, if he doesn't look after them, make great decisions on their behalf and ultimately make them feel happy and secure then he runs the risk of ending up with no business to support anyone, least himself. I only wish I had discovered this fact earlier on in my career as the implications to a salesperson of knowing that a customer HAS to make great decisions on his staff's behalf, alternatively he puts the good of his company, staff and immediate family at huge risk.

Now that we have identified this, and know the implications of him making a bad decision, your question should be, is he really the right person to ask? Who are best qualified to ask whether a piece of machinery is going to make work practices easier? Who are the best people to ask whether a new software platform will make accounting more accurate? Indeed it is his staff, so surely we need to be asking them?

I am not proposing you directly ask each individual for their reactions to your product or service, but wouldn't it be great if you could get the customer, business owner or CEO to answer you with what they would each say? Think about it for a second, if a **CEO says that four members of his staff would benefit from your product or service, what position does that put him in if he now turns round and declines your offer**? Doesn't that make him a bad boss? Will this cause a sense of guilt if he knows he could have made them happier and more productive?

It is this very fact that not many salespeople have ever really thought about and very few have ever used to their advantage but now when we piece this all together you will be able to utilize it to your advantage.

Key Point: We all buy products or services for others, even though we cannot see the benefit of it ourselves because we all want the praise in giving.

What have you bought your partner that you could see no benefit of?

See Their Happiness

Quick Summary
What we have found so far is that during the working day, the customer's family at home is replaced by his employees, and he has a duty to them as they provide his immediate family with the life they have. Secondly we have seen that by using a name of someone you know in a story plays a hugely influential part as it attaches images, feeling and emotions.

Your first and most important objective throughout the course of your sales presentation is to ask for the names of staff members, suppliers and key customers so that you can include and attach them to your product or service when providing your solution.

Scenario 1:
You: "So you are buying this car as a surprise for your wife?"
Customer: "It's her birthday present."
You: "Just out of interest, what is her name?"
Customer: "Sue, or Susan if I'm mad at her."
You: "Well I think Sue is going to be absolutely overwhelmed with this little sports car. It has a fully automatic retractable roof, air conditioning and ABS brakes. What do you think? Can you see Sue driving up the highway with the wind in her hair and a big smile on her face? What a fantastic present for her."

What images do you have of Sue? How old is Sue? What color hair does she have? Do you know anyone like Sue?

As the salesperson what do you know about Sue other than the fact your customer calls her Susan when he's mad? Absolutely nothing. It is the customer who has the close relationship with his wife and it is he who creates the images in his head and feels the emotion of pleasing her. What happens in reality is that your customer nods his head, puts a smile on his face and has visualized his wife's reaction (future outcome) to his generosity. All you had to do was to make the story a personal one. How would he feel if you say the car is sold and take the offer away?

Scenario 2:
You: "What are the names of the people who will be using this software?"
Customer: "Steve and Janet."
You: "Ok, so at the moment then if a customer inquiry comes in to Steve am I right in thinking that to get the customer's details on screen he has to locate the folder, find the right section, locate that customer's file, search for previous invoices, check with dispatch before he can answer the question?"
Customer: "Um… Sounds about right."
You: "In that case this is going to make Steve very happy. The software will bring all these details up on screen while Steve is talking to the customer therefore he doesn't need to get in a panic. It means he doesn't have to work as hard, makes him far more efficient and generally a lot happier because all of the information he needs is at hand. How do you think Steve would feel about that?"

Again do you have any form of relationship with Steve? Have you ever met Steve before? What do you need to know about him? All you do know is that the customer visualized Steve struggling to get the information he requires to make sure the customer is happy, he saw Steve being a lot happier and then told you that Steve would feel great about it.

Consider the two statements below:

1: It was really horrible to see him like that. He was working flat out for 12 hours a day, the sweat was pouring from his brow and he looked as if he was just about to collapse with exhaustion. It really wasn't the person I knew. We went back again 6 months later and were completely amazed as the old machinery had gone and they had replaced it with all new equipment which made it so much easier for him. He just looked fresher, his humor was back and he had a huge smile on his face. It was really good to see him back.

Before considering statement 2 I would like you to insert one of your parents' name where you see (XXXX).

2: It was really horrible to see him like that. (XXXX) was working flat out for 12 hours a day, the sweat was pouring from his brow and he looked like he was just about to collapse with exhaustion. He really wasn't the (XXXX) I knew. We went back again 6 months later and were completely amazed as the old machinery had gone and they had replaced it with all new equipment which had made it so much easier for him. (XXXX) just looked fresher, his humor was back and he had a huge smile on his face. It was really good to see the old (XXXX) back.

What changed from statement 1 to statement 2? For most the inclusion of your father's name made the statement far more personal and where in statement 1 there were little or no pictures formed in your mind, in statement 2 you had images of your father slaving away, sweating and generally not liking the work. How does that make you feel knowing that someone could do that to your father? In the end though you would have seen you father, less stressed and how you want to see him, with a huge smile on his face back to his old self.

The only differences here are first, the inclusion of your father's name, but more importantly the images and emotions that his name created in your minds eye.

Key Point: When you know the person in the story it becomes very personal, vivid and almost impossible to detach yourself from the emotion.

The Answer Is Out There

A couple of questions for you to consider.

1: When making a purchase do you generally commit based on past experience, present state of mind or future benefits?

2: Fill in the blanks:
Bad experiences happen in the _____.
Good experiences happen in the _____.

The biggest deciding factor for most people when committing to a purchase is the future benefits of the product. Consider the car being bought for Sue. **The biggest motivator for the customer to purchase the car is how Sue will look ONCE she owns it.** How it will make her feel ONCE he delivers it to her and how he will be treated ONCE her birthday is over. All of these considerations are future based outcomes. The same would be true for buying a new house. When you first look around a new property that you are considering buying your thoughts are led by, where will everyone sleep, is the garden large enough for entertaining, and would your furniture fit in this room. **You imagine** a life in that house with your belongings and your family inside, all of which are in the future.

In question two, most will opt for "bad" being in the past and "good" being in the future. This is why as a salesperson you may have been to a customer's premises where realistically they should not still be in business because of their financial status or a therapist sees a client whose marriage is all but over. Both of these customers believe that something good is going to happen to them in the future, which will change their fortunes and enable them to live their dreams.

Dreams, Aspirations, Goals and Objectives are all based in the future. So much of our lives are directed towards future based outcomes that if used in stories relating to your product or service will appeal to the customers buying motives to ensure he gets where he needs to be.

Key Point: Customers look at details when considering committing TODAY and look at benefits when considering whether to commit in the FUTURE.

Fear Of Losing

It is generally thought by most sales professionals that if you add something to an offer and make it more attractive that there is a better chance of getting the order or commitment. In many cases this is true, however is it the most effective or powerful way?

What if you were to take something away or show the customer that by not going ahead with your proposal they would indeed lose something or experience a sense of pain? What would be the outcome?

Which is your biggest motivator?

Scenario 1: It is your birthday and someone has kindly given you a one-dollar 'Lotto' card as a present. Ten minutes before the weekly draw they tell you that they are feeling lucky and ask you if you'd swap it back to them for a dollar. Do you swap it?

Scenario 2: You are offered two investment funds by an advisor who is advising where to place your ENTIRE life's savings. The first has a capped gain of 25% and a capped loss of 25% over the course of a year and the other has an unlimited gain and a potential 100% loss in the course of a year. Which one would you choose?

Research has shown that a large majority of people would rather keep the 'Lotto' card instead of a one dollar gain and would rather take the safer investment fund of a capped 25% growth against a potential unlimited gain on investment.

In both cases the underlying motivator here is the fear of loss or the fear of pain. Imagine swapping that card for the sum of one dollar and then the person won the jackpot of 7 million dollars. How would that make you feel? Rather than experiencing that potential pain however small, people will generally not swap the card in fear of it winning.

The same set of emotional feelings are used when deciding which investment fund to place your ENTIRE life savings in. The thought of unlimited growth is an appealing offering but when offset with a potential loss of everything, how PAINFUL would that loss be? Little consideration would have been given to what would happen if the investment had quadrupled in size in a year because the fear of the potential loss of everything was over-powering.

Finally, consider this important point. You have a chance of betting your house on the spin of a roulette wheel. If it comes in red you get to keep your house plus you'll win the value of your house in cash. If it comes in black you win nothing and you lose your house. Do you place a bet?

Was the pain of losing everything too great to outweigh the gains?

Key Point: People are highly motivated to reduce, wherever possible, the feelings of pain or loss even if there are big gains at stake.

Piecing Together

We now have all the necessary parts of the puzzle for you to literally buy back what it is you are offering to your customer. To show how this is best used we will look at ways of using it in specific industries, which you can adapt to suit your own business and needs.

The Objective

The objective in using this method is to allow your customer the luxury of visualizing what it is going to be like to use your product in the future. We want to enable him to literally feel and see the positive emotions of his staff when he presents to them the services that you have provided. **Then and only then are you going to take that away from him and give him back what he already owns and in turn induce the fear of loss/pain.** This is truly brilliant.

Software Provider:
In the course of your questioning of the customer you are looking to identify the following things.

1: Staff names who will benefit from your software.
(Who are the managers of those departments? Adam)

2: Names of key customers and/or suppliers.
(What's the name of someone Adam would deal with regularly? Debbie)

3: How are they currently operating including difficulties and stresses?
(So they have to do X then Y and then Z before they can answer Q?)

Once you have the above information you can incorporate them into your presentation.

1: The use of staff and customer names in feature/benefit stories.
("Adam will love this." "This will make it so easy for Debbie.")

2: Use emotions to indicate what is being done and how it will be in the future.
("Instead of Adam struggling to find X…" "How happy will Debbie be if…?")

3: Relate your stories to the future outcome.
("After the installation we can..." "In three months time Adam will be able to...")

4: Get commitment from the customer in the form of what his staff would say.
("Do you think this would help Adam?" "Can you see the improvements for Debbie?" "Could Debbie use this product?" "How would Adam like it if...?")

Are you with me so far? We are now just about ready to present the price of your product and then buy it back!

When Executing The Buy Back, Be Descriptive and Attach Emotion

You: "That will be $25,000 in total, but before you make up your mind let me put it another way. Let's imagine that you have had the installation and have been using the product for six months. Adam has now got a big smile on his face and isn't half as stressed as he used to be. Queries are now processed so much quicker, all your staff have thanked you for having it installed and Debbie your top customer is delighted that now her orders are getting placed automatically only for me to come back in six months time and offer you a check for $25,000 to take it all away and place you right back to where you are now, doing what you've always done. You'd tell me to keep it wouldn't you?"
Customer: "Well, yeah."

In practice you can include so many more staff members' names, suppliers' names, current complications and future benefits in your 'buy back' story. To get this to have the impact it deserves you now need to re-read the above 'buy back' and replace Debbie and Adam with the names of kids, family or friends who mean a lot to you and notice the difference.

Real Estate

The same information steps need to be followed as above, getting family and friends' names. Once you have these you are going to include them in your presentation stories detailing how they are feeling at the moment and what a huge difference it is going to make when they purchase the property.

Remember to include emotions and names then relate them all to the future outcome.

Buy Back

You: "I think you'll agree that this is a lot of house for the $350,000 asking price but before you go away today let me try to put the money side of things a different way. Let's go out a year from now. Gareth would be what 10 now and Nina 8, is that right?"
Customer: "Yeah that's correct."
You: "Ok so a year from now, the kids aren't having to share a tiny bedroom, Gareth is outside with you Dave, playing ball with you here in the back yard. You can see Nina and Kelly laughing excitedly through the French windows preparing the food for the barbecue with your friends this evening. The kids are excited, the weather's perfect and you're really looking forward to it.

What if I were to walk in at that precise moment and offer you your $350,000 back in exchange for your old house where the kids were sharing a room, all treading on each other's toes, no back yard and no barbecue? Come on it wouldn't happen would it?"

Again I should stress that these examples are simply to give you a flavor of how to deliver and the type of story that you need to tell.

Trainer / Coach

Buy Back

You: "Ok, so that is $1000 per delegate per day plus a speaking fee of $2500 and expenses of $1500 which in total comes to $12000. What I'd like to do is explain this is in a slightly different way. You said earlier that you have not had much luck with material other trainers have shared with your sales team and in particular Gerry your manager and that he felt that there wasn't much benefit in taking his team off the road if the material wasn't new. Is that correct?"
Customer: "Yes that right."
You: "That's fine. But I'm going to paint you a picture of your sales team in 3 months; having completed our course and utilizing all that we have proposed today: Katarena, your top saleswoman has smashed her targets by 40%, Stefan your current number two is now performing better that he ever has and has just bought his dream Porsche. The company profits have risen 30% on the previous quarter and Gerry is just a different guy. He's laughing, relaxed, and is really enjoying heading up the team. Now I'll come back at the end of the 3 months and offer you $12,000 to take away your team's new found knowledge, put Gerry back exactly where he is now and wipe 30% off of the company profits. Come on, you'd never let that happen for $12,000, would you?"

Summary

Well there you are. This is how YOU can literally buy back the very offering you are proposing to your customers or clients.
   It is such an easy technique that you can literally start using it tomorrow, once you have learnt and understood the core components of how and why it works:

1: Gather and use as many names personal to the customer as you can.

2: Place those people in your stories, detailing the hardships they face now and the happy outcomes into the future once your product or service is being used. Be intensely descriptive.

3: Place all of your stories in the future tense and show the customer how his employees are going to FEEL about your product or service and more importantly about him. Attach plenty of emotion.

4: Deliver your price and then use ALL of the information that you gathered to show him exactly what a benefit buying from you is by BUYING BACK your product in the future.

Take the price of this book. This one chapter makes you a better influencer and persuader by 20% because you use this one technique; then I come back in 6 months and erase your memory of ever having read it and I give you the price you paid back. Come on, I think you'd give me a lot worse than a polite "no thank you". Wouldn't you?

Chapter Two

Power Farming for Sales

Question: *Would you trust a real estate agent to promote your property without having him first look around it?*

If you said yes to the question, then you are part of a very small minority because generally speaking clients will want the agent to know exactly what to promote and what to stay away from. In saying that I have had experience of agents who have looked round a property, know what the great features of that property are but still end up being glorified key holders in opening the door and waiting for ME to have a good look round. Totally inept!

The point of the question was to identify whether you believed it was possible to sell a product or service effectively if you have not seen or experienced what the customers' current situation or equipment is.

In this chapter you will learn how, when and why it is absolutely imperative to survey or tour the clients' premises to identify needs, possible solutions and current hardships felt by employees and how to use the staff members in helping you sell to the decision maker.

Good Morning

The time is 10 a.m.; you have an appointment to see a CEO of a print and design company about changing his major print machine. The drive there has been uneventful, the sun is shining and in general you are feeling pretty good and confident of getting a sale. You arrive outside of the customers' premises and walk into the reception area. A lady looks at you and greets you with, "Good morning, how may I help?"

This chapter is all about using the environment, staff members and human nature to get the very best chance of securing that order TODAY. The techniques and strategies in this chapter can be used in any selling situation whether it is direct sales, retail sales or even as a consumer yourself.

Employing THEIR Staff

I want to start by asking you a quick question. Would you close more orders and increase you sales on the day IF you had the companies own employees on your side trying to sell your product for you?

What a perfect selling situation. Imagine a Chief Mechanic telling the CEO that your product is not only ideal for what he needs but also is very reasonably priced. I think you'll agree that by simply having that other person selling with you will enormously increase your chances of getting the order. But how often does this happen? Probably not often enough in your experience until now.

Sowing the Seeds

Remember earlier, "Good morning, how may I help?" This is where your sales presentation begins. I'm sure you have all had tips given to you about addressing receptionists or switchboard operators but have you ever been told to employ them as your selling aid?

On being welcomed to that business you need to start your covert selling immediately!

[Ed. Note- Covert selling refers to subtle, unseen and intentional strategic persuasion.]

Authority Check

More than likely you will have the name and position of the person you are just about to meet but how certain are you of the information you have been given? Have you ever carried out one of your best presentations only to find out the person you have spent the last two hours with cannot make a final decision because they are only a department manager? Very frustrating!

This then is your first opportunity to make sure you have the right person to make the right type of decision.

Receptionist: "Good morning, how may I help?"
You: "Hello, I'm Gary from ABC Print. I have an appointment at 10:30 with David May."
Receptionist: "Ok, I'll just inform him that you are here and waiting."

STOP!!! This is going exactly the way all of your presentations have gone. You need to ask a very simple question BEFORE she contacts David.

You: "Before you do, can I just check that David is the CEO isn't he?"
Receptionist: "Yes he is."
You: "Great, thank you"

I am embarrassed about how easy and completely obvious this question is but I know how many salespeople have never even thought about asking or simply never bothered. The information you have just gathered has saved you two hours of your valuable time talking to a potential time waster.

Whether you are meeting with a CEO of a multi-national, an IT specialist or an accountant it really doesn't matter what selling situation you find yourself in. The fact remains that if you do not ask early on in your communication who your contact really is then you run the risk of wasting your time, giving good information to someone who can't actually make a decision and ensuring you hear the objection, "I need to run this past X".

$10,000 Key Point: Never assume that your contact holds the position you think they do. Always question someone BEFORE you meet him or her and save yourself wasting your valuable time.

Praise Them

This is something that many of you will find difficult to do because you have either never been told to do it or worse told never to talk about it.

I want to cast your minds back to a favorite vacation of yours. You had a really good time, had time to relax, spend time with the family and make some new friends. The weather was absolutely beautiful, the scenery was stunning and your photos show you being really happy.

Doesn't that just sound perfect?

Now, how good was it really? Was it as perfect as you think and was it how you communicated it when asked?

I know you must be thinking, "Well of course it was. What are you getting at?"

Ok, I'll come clean and explain where we are going with this. The vacation above really might have been a truly perfect time and something you'll cherish forever with your memories and photo. The problem is that you didn't quite explain it like this when asked by family members, colleagues or clients.

A strange part of human behavior is for us not to come across as conceited or smug, we will go some lengths not to be portrayed in this manner.

Still don't believe me? Below I will show you something that you've always done, will probably find hard to change and how to use it to your advantage.

Scenario:

Colleague: "Hi, Kat how was your vacation? Did you have a good time?"

You: "Yes thank you it was absolutely perfect and nice to get away from work for a while"

Colleague: "Was it Italy you went to?"

You: "Yes, Lake Garda." (I can personally recommend this, it's beautiful.)

Colleague: "Oh, I'd love to go to Italy. I heard the scenery is gorgeous, the coffee is amazing and the food is out of this world. You are so lucky."

You: "Yes we were and it really is beautiful however it isn't cheap. The cost of a single coffee was $12 a cup and the food although nice was simply over priced."

There you go you couldn't help yourself, could you? You could just expect that someone might feel that you are luckier than they are and therefore you felt dutiful to respond with a list of negatives to counter balance your embarrassment of their praise.

Am I off on this scenario? Absolutely not! You probably have done this every single day of your life.

A client comments on how nice your car is and how he would love to have one just like it and comments how lucky you are. So what do you do....? You say something like "Yeah, it drives really well and I'm really pleased with it except the servicing costs are a bit high and its had to go back to the dealer twice to get a fault rectified."

STOP IT.... STOP IT NOW!

I can't resist it. This is the thing that it appears everyone does when questioned except no one would actually admit it in the open.

You and your partner have a date to meet a group of friends that you haven't seen for a while. The food was lovely and the wine is flowing rather too well. An old friend pulls you to one side and engages you into a conversation.

Friend: "You look so happy Kat. You are so lucky to have met Gary he seems such a lovely person."

WARNING! If you are sitting next to your partner then be sure not to smile or else you'll have to explain this next part to them.

Kat: "Yeah he is but you don't have to live with him 24/7."

Why do you say this? Why couldn't you just accept the nice words and be done with it. The reason you couldn't is because you can't. How would you feel if you were just to take the compliment and nod knowingly? The chances are you would feel uncomfortable and feel that if you didn't address the balance on praise vs. criticism scale you would be seen in a bad light.

Key Point: We do not take compliments well. On receiving a compliment we are compelled to repay it with a criticism to address the uncomfortable balance caused by the praise.

What we will now do is have a look at how this strategy can be utilized in a selling environment because when done right it will have huge implications.

Remember at this stage we are still in the waiting area with only the receptionist to talk to. How can you use this with them?

Scenario 1:
You: "Can I ask what make of computer you are currently using?"
Receptionist: "It says it's a CompuPC."
You: "Ah ok, I've heard very good reports about those. I've been told they are generally really reliable, well equipped and affordable."
Receptionist: "Yeah it seems to be a good machine although you occasionally get a blue screen and you have to re-boot it."

Now, consider whether you would have ever got this sort of information from the CEO or IT specialist and now that you do have it how powerful it will be when comparing to your product. Could you possibly use this information later in your presentation when talking to the CEO?

Scenario 2:
You: "As a kid I always wanted to be a lawyer. I've always imagined it being such an interesting job to do. Meeting people, investigating cases, preparing for court, you're so lucky to have a job that's so varied."
Lawyer: "Yeah it does have its plus points but it isn't exactly like you described. The hours can be horrendous and the cases can often be quite laborious."

Now wasn't that just so easy. Imagine you are selling a new software package, recruitment services or even office furniture. The information you have just attained is something that would never be given to you in the course of a normal sales presentation. Every one of these products can be and should be linked to the negative feedback you have now just been given by making this lawyer's job easier, make him more efficient and improve his work surroundings.

Key Point: The Praise vs. Criticism technique enables you to attain information that you would ordinarily not be privy to. Keep it, log it and definitely use it.

The Rumor Mill

Take your average sales appointment. How many employees in that company know who you are, what you are doing there, who you work for and what products you sell?

The chances are that there are very few people who will know the answers to the above questions. But hang on a minute, who are the people who are ultimately going to benefit from your product, service and ideas? The piece of machinery you sell, the personal investment plans, protective clothing or computer network are all for the benefit of the employees and often do not even affect the CEO in any way, shape or form. In a previous chapter you learnt how the CEO / Decision maker isn't really the right person to get a decision from at all and that relating your product towards staff members has the greatest impact.

What then would be a likely outcome if those very same employees were to know in advance who you were, what you sold and how it would make their roles easier? Add to that, if they had a forum to comment to the CEO on why they believe YOUR product would be ideal for them and even suggest to him that he should buy it.

Before we can facilitate this forum you are going to have to do some work whilst in the reception orwaiting area and sow the seeds that will grow while you are presenting your product, service or idea so that it will blossom just when you require them.

Why Are You Here?

Most receptionists or switchboard operators or even people who just greet you at the door have little or no idea who you are or why you are there. As I mentioned earlier, this is a shame because if only they knew what your product, service or idea was and how it would affect their day to day working lives then there would be a good chance that they would want to make your acquaintance and question you about your meeting.

Who then is the one person who is "normally" labeled as the office gossip? Who do you go to to find out the real reason Kelly's been signed off sick? In most instances it is the person you stand in front of at reception.

This is where our biggest and most effective seeds get sown for to prime the receptionist with why you are there and what you are looking to achieve almost ensures your name will get mentioned to someone. (I guarantee this in the next section.)

Scenario:

You: "Hello, I'm Gary from ABC Print. I have an appointment at 10:30 with David May."
Receptionist: "Ok, I'll just inform him that you are here and waiting."
You: "Before you do, can I just check that David is the CEO isn't he?"
Receptionist: "Yes he is."
You: "Great, thank you."
Receptionist: "He'll be with you in 5 minutes if you'd just like to wait."
You: "Ok that's fine. By the way did David explain why I was here?"
Receptionist: "I rarely get told about any of his meetings."
You: "Oh right, David has invited me in to have a look at replacing your 4 color printer. Apparently you've had it for 5 years now. Who is it that runs that machine?"

This conversation will run for the next five minutes but the seed has already been planted. Let's review what has been said and what words have been chosen.

1: You: "Ok that's fine. By the way did David explain why I was here?"
Receptionist: "I rarely get told about any of his meetings."

This person rarely gets the good information first hand. You have just offered it to them on a plate and will divulge your meeting plans.

2: You: "Oh right, David has invited me in to have a look at replacing your 4 color printer to speed up you print time by 30%. Apparently you've had it for 5 years now. Who is it that runs that machine?"

The word "invited" is absolutely imperative for this technique to work. Whether your company made a cold call to the prospect or whether they called you, the fact is that there would have been a discussion and possible negotiation over when and where you were to have the meeting. This in effect is inviting you to meet at a time convenient to both your client and yourself and so is a true "invitation".

This is all well and good but the person you are telling will never hear the word "invited" and interpret it in the way we have just described. On hearing the word "invite" the receptionist will hear that their CEO, their BOSS and the person they owe a job to has had a good idea, contacted you and invited you in. Here lies the seed in which will develop a beautiful blossom bearing fruits of orders.

Once you have sown the seed you are going to briefly explain why you are there and ask a couple of information gathering questions. This will ensure that if asked, the receptionist or switchboard operator has all the information they need to spread the word of your meeting.

What are the chances of the receptionist telling someone you are there and what you are purposing? Quite high I would suggest however next we will almost guarantee it.

Key Point: Explaining who you are and what you are there for will often result in your meeting becoming public knowledge.

Good Morning

So there you are waiting to be lead into a board or meeting room and for most this is a time to either calm your nerves, work out what you are going to say or get that last trip to the bathroom out of the way.

Not for you though! You have some seeds that need sowing before you go anywhere.

The reception or waiting area of most companies acts as a hub for employees to either have a quick chat with the switchboard operator, hand over some outgoing post or to let them know they are coming in or out of the premises. In my experience this is a place of activity with people coming and going throughout the time you are there. With that in mind I have two questions for you.

1: How many people have you said good morning or afternoon to whilst you have been waiting for your contact?

2: How many times have you been working at a company, seen someone sat or stood in the waiting area and asked someone who they are and what they are doing there?

Let's address the second one first with an example.

A stranger has parked outside of your home. Do you walk through the door and ask your partner who they are and whether they know them?

Another stranger is walking around your company with your CEO. Have you ever asked a colleague who they are and whether they are a new member of staff?

It is our inherent need to question that you are going to use to sow your second seed.

When waiting in the reception or waiting room, rather that just standing there or worse still sitting down reading a company brochure, you are going to be saying hello and good morning to any person who comes within five paces of you. The simple act of a smile and a nice greeting will create enough curiosity for them to feel compelled to ask someone who you are and why you are there.

Key Point: Curiosity will compel people to ask who you are IF you greet them in a friendly and enthusiastic way.

Section Summary

All that has been learned so far has been while you have been waiting in reception and BEFORE you have met you business contact. We have sown some seeds that the next section will make flourish but for now I want to do a quick review.

1: Never assume that your contact holds the position you think they do. Always question someone BEFORE you meet him or her and save yourself wasting your valuable time.

2: We do not take compliments well. On receiving a compliment we are compelled to repay it with a criticism to address the uncomfortable balance caused by the praise.

3: Explaining who you are and why you are there will often result in your meeting becoming public knowledge.

4: Curiosity will compel people to ask who you are IF you greet them in a friendly and enthusiastic way.

In this section I have sown the seeds for you to use later on in your presentation when you will be able to stand back, relax and have someone else do your selling for you. It's brilliant because it's you who still gets paid!

Picking The Fruit

How often do you survey your customers' premises? Do you need to survey their premises? What good or harm would it do?

In this section we will discover the importance of surveying your customers' site. Whether you are in insurance, security, furniture, software, clothing, machinery or stationery there is not a good reason why you shouldn't have a good look round the company but there are some very good reasons why you absolutely should.

Out Into The Field

One of the most important facets of surveying the clients' site is to remove your client out of his natural environment. The domain of your CEO is his office or boardroom. It is in this room where he controls all lines of communication, passes or rubbishes all ideas, installs fear into his staff and generally runs his business.

Is it feasible then that you as a salesperson are going to get the respect and time you deserve IF you conduct your meeting in HIS control tower? The answer to this is probably not and to a degree you'll end up being treated either as just another salesperson or even like a staff member, neither of these is ideal for your message to be received in the way you are intending.

There is one place in which he and you will feel more comfortable and where you will get treated with respect and interest. That place is whilst walking around his business and for good reason. Firstly he will not want to be seen by his staff in a bad light and so will be showing off about his company and secondly it is almost impossible to walk next to someone side by side and not say anything! This lends itself very easily for you to control the topic of conversation.

So far so good, except for one small but very important point.

Key Point: If you ask to survey the site you will often be told that they do not have time, there is no need or worse they will get someone else to show you 'round.

What we need is a technique that ensures you get a survey and the decision maker walks with you, which leads us nicely on to our next point.

Get Up, Get On Up, and Really DO THIS

Can you remember the last time you visited a restaurant with a group of friends? The food was delicious, the wine was plentiful and the company was superb. The time is 23:30 and you are all now sat round the table sharing the good old stories of yesteryear and sipping your double espressos when a couple of friends stand up, push their chairs back and announce that they are going to call it a night as it is late. What happens next?

In so many cases that I have been in like this, the act of someone saying they are going will normally cause the rest of the group to get up and leave as well bringing the night to a polite ending.

Why did that happen? The fact that they took action without first asking permission suggested that what they said is exactly what they intended doing. They didn't put it up for discussion nor did they ask permission. So to ensure you get a survey and with the decision maker we are going to utilize this phenomena to our advantage.

When you feel the time is right to do a survey of the company all you need to do is push you chair back, make your way to a standing position whilst telling them that as part of your service or role you need to have a quick look round.

On doing this you will notice that the customer's body language instantly changes because now he feels compelled to acknowledge and act on your request. It's as simple as that!

This technique will work even better if you suggest a reason for having to do a survey. (Locate existing equipment; find out where something is, etc.)

Read through the last paragraph again as you might have just forgotten it! Still works!

Cultivating Your Seeds

Did you bury your seeds deep enough? Because this is when we are going to see how well they have grown.

It's now been an hour since you left the company and comfort of the reception area. Unknown to you a member of staff who you gave a wonderful greeting to has since been back to reception and asked the receptionist who you were and what you were doing there. The receptionist could only give them what you had told her which was, that you were INVITED in to talk about replacing the 4-color printer, which apparently will save them 30% in time.

This person will then without doubt go back to their desk and tell someone else that they are getting a new printer, which is going to speed everything up. Not only that but they believe you were asked to come in because the CEO felt he needed one. Within one hour of you mentioning this little point you can bet that at least half the company know why you are there and what you are looking to do.

To put this into a different context, imagine that you are told by a third party that someone was meeting your CEO to discuss the possibilities of setting up a sales meeting in Hawaii. How soon would the whole company know?

OK, back to our company tour.

What chance is there if you are looking around the print shop with the CEO of someone stopping you and asking about when they are getting their new printer? What if you were to ask a member of staff a question about the current printer knowing that there is a good chance of them hearing the rumor? What if you know that they will want to please the boss by letting him know that they know of his fantastic idea to get you in?

WIN! WIN! WIN!

This is when all your sowing earlier pays off because now the employees are involved and have shown great interest in your product, service and ideas.

You have just pushed the 'work family' protection and pleasure button to which we already know is the reason the boss HAS to make good decisions.

Key Point*: Stop and question existing employees as you never know, they might know something!*

Giving Invitations

When in the reception area you asked the receptionist for the name of the person who looks after the piece of machinery, pension fund, IT equipment or whatever else you are presenting. It is now that you are going to use this piece of information and pull off an amazing feat.

On surveying your clients' premises you will eventually come to the very people with whom your product is most aligned. You can assume so long as you had sown your seeds correctly that they already know why you are there and so it is now more than ever that you need to ask a couple of questions as to who runs the department and how it currently operates. This will allow this person to ask you whether you are there because of (X) reason and maybe suggest that it is even a good idea. Remember the CEO is with you throughout the tour!

Key Point: *As a parting gesture and because you know how this will benefit them you are going to INVITE them into your presentation with the approval of the CEO.*

Now, should the CEO agree to your kind gesture I need to prepare you with what WILL happen.

2's Company – 3's Perfect

You are now sitting in a meeting consisting of the CEO, an employee responsible for what you are selling and yourself.

This is where all your Christmas's come at once as without a shadow of a doubt I do not know a better way of securing an order for any product, anywhere!

Your job now is to present your product, service or idea detailing how it can improve upon what they have in place currently, affect efficiency and improve profits but you are going to do it in a very specific way.

With the CEO and an invitee it is important that you present to them in such a way that they play their own specific roles.

$10,000 Key Point:
1: Present your feature and benefits to them both
2: Ask for an opinion from the invited guest

Scenario:
You (to both): "The first benefit you'll take advantage of is………"
You (to guest): "Can you see how that would improve upon X?"

You (to both): "This is how we speed up the process of………"
You (to guest): "I'm sure your guys would be happy with that wouldn't they?"

Now I will explain exactly what is happening in this scenario and how with precision you have created the perfect environment.

1: You quite rightly told the receptionist that you had been invited in.

2: You said hello to everyone who came within five paces of you.

3: One or more people questioned who you were and why you were there.

4: A rumor went around the company that the CEO had a great idea to change X.

5: You went out to survey the site and get him out of his control tower.

6: You questioned staff members who in turn questioned you.

7: On meeting the manager of the department you invited them into your meeting.

8: You presented your product and sought opinions of the invited person.

Major Key Point: *Remember the person you have invited into your meeting BELIEVES that the CEO has invited you there. In front of the CEO you are asking for opinions from them. Are they ever going to say NO I don't like it IF it was their CEO's initial idea to look at changing what they already have in place?*

The invited guest will NEVER say no to anything you present for fear of offending their CEO or manager and therefore they become an agent helping you to sell your product and they never know what they are doing.

I promised you at the start of the chapter that you could literally employ your prospective client's own staff to act in your best interests.

Have fun with this because it will make you more money that you currently make IF you follow the plan in sowing the seeds, watching them blossom and then picking the fruit.

Chapter Three

Focusing Their Thoughts

Now let's get one thing straight right away; I guess you are wondering why I have mis-spelled the word "focusing"?

It is a purposeful and deliberate mistake made only to come back to a bit later on.

This is what you've all been waiting for, the secrets the truly brilliant sales people and organizations of this world never wanted you to know. How to manipulate your customer's thinking and actions in the direction you need them to be: towards your products, your services and your ideas.

Ethically Correct?

Before we start I should ask you a question: Do you believe the manipulation of someone's thoughts and actions is ethically correct?

If your answer was NO then please read no further. For all you lucky people who said, "Yeah sure", then you're going to learn some great stuff. You are going to understand exactly what your customer is thinking at anytime, how to direct and mis-direct their thought patterns. You will literally be able to steer their thoughts and actions away from whatever you don't want them to think or do.

It's As Simple As That!

Let me first direct your thoughts towards my stand on manipulating people. In order to make it crystal clear I would like you to answer a couple more quick questions and then I'll share my thoughts with you.

1: A child is playing in the street. A car approaches from around the corner and at its current speed is likely to hit the child. Do you intervene in whatever way you can to manipulate the situation?

2: Place one hand or a piece of paper over the page above this line. Go on just play the game for me.

Now, what did you read BEFORE you read, "It's as simple as that!"?

3: A friend is going on a date with someone whom you know to be a total liar and a compulsive cheat. Do you tell your friend about that person?

4: A customer has no need and will get zero benefit from the purchase of your product. Do you still sell it to them using your newfound knowledge?

Question 1: Ok, so did you answer, "Yes"? I personally would do whatever I could to manipulate the situation so that the child is out of harm's way and remains safe. This, I have no problem with at all as it was in the best interest of the child for me to change the course of his actions.

Question 2: We'll get to this one once we've answered the others.

Question 3: I'd feel compelled to tell my friend about the person they are going to spend an evening, if not more, with since I feel an ethical responsibility for those I respect, love and care for. I really couldn't let my friend befriend such a person knowing that they could potentially get hurt especially when I knew they didn't need to.

Question 4: This one I have a really big problem with! I would certainly never make someone part with their hard earned money for something that they didn't want, didn't need or couldn't afford. My upbringing and integrity means that in order to sleep easy I need to be safe in the knowledge that my customers are better off now than before I met them. I do have an ethical responsibility to the people I sell to otherwise I become nothing more than a legalized mugger!

There you go; a quick insight into why I believe that to manipulate someone in thought or in action has its place ONLY if it is for the GOOD of that person and will ultimately be something that they look back on and thank you for.

Do You Know Your Own Mind?

I am sure, like me, that you are of the opinion that you make your own decisions; take your own actions with little or no influence from the outside world. Unfortunately, this couldn't be further from the truth as we will discover and you will read in the upcoming chapter on Role Projection.

Why then have we got this view of decision-making and how could it be possible for others to make decisions for us IF we believe they didn't have an influence?

This, in part, was the very basis from which all my sales knowledge and research came. I couldn't accept that I was not as individual as I thought I was and had in many ways played out a life that others had made for me and taken actions that I (if I had known) might not have taken.

In this chapter I want you to understand how you are being constantly influenced by media and people and in turn how you can influence your customers, clients, family and friends.

My goal is not to make this a theory driven chapter, explaining complicated neurological detail or psychological process but something that you can have a bit of fun with both in home and office environments.

You're Lazy

Don't take this too personally but your brain is very lazy and doesn't like to be worked too hard if there is an easier route available. As an example of this can you recall your school days or more recent training sessions where in the beginning you were quite happy listening to whatever was being taught? Everything was going great until they started talking about things that either you had no interest in or you didn't really understand. For most of us, this is when our brain just gives up trying to pay attention and we now enter our brain's own little dream world.

Our brains literally give up trying to stay focused. Did you ever in the course of that lesson or during the training session think consciously to yourself, "I'm going to enter my own thoughts and daydream about something more exciting than this until he either spots me or stops talking nonsense." (I've just offended every manager I've ever had!) You had no control over where your brain went, it just turned off. After the lesson or course had finished, you could no longer remember anything that was taught after your brain switched itself into "Stand By" mode.

Another area in which our brains let us down is when we are asked for opinions or answers to questions. The job of thinking of an in-depth answer seems too difficult, particularly when presented with an easier option. To understand this we first need to answer the questions below.

Question 1: What are your plans for the next two years?

Question 2: What are your plans for the next two years? For example do you want to earn more money, get a bigger house or even drive a better car?

For your brain to answer question 1 is actually quite hard if you haven't got a nailed on career or personal plan. The question is too ambiguous and is too vast for your brain to pin point what it is you actually want. Oh and before we move on we should address the fact that we probably don't even know what our plans are but because someone asked we feel we have a duty to give a logical and plausible answer. More on this later!

41

The answer to question 2 was so much easier for your poor little brain to cope with as you were given three very good and justifiable goals for the next two years. I would imagine that most of you included some of those goals in your answer, which tells me that rather than think about all the possibilities your brain simply went… "Those answers seem pretty good so I'll use them as a start."

This is amazing when you consider all the answers that you could have given.

Key Point: *Our brains do not like to be worked too hard if there are easier routes to a solution or if not stimulated by a topic of communication.*

These very character traits are what we will be exploiting to delete messages, direct thoughts and have people take actions that they wouldn't normally take.

Are You Listening To Me?

Have you ever been speaking to someone and thought to yourself; "I shouldn't have said that?" If so, then wouldn't it have been great if you could have that person forget you ever made the comment giving you time to replace it with something else if only to remind them later?

In ten minutes that's exactly what you'll be able to do.

Earlier I asked you four questions about the ethics of manipulating thoughts and actions. Question 2 asked you to place your hand over the page and remember what you had just read.

Be honest, did you have problems remembering what you had only just read? If so then you are in the vast majority because when asked almost everyone will have some difficulty recalling the information. Why is that?

The reasons for this are actually very simple and very easy to learn but before we look at the technique I first need to give some explanation.

It's As Simple As That!

Remember when you placed your hand or paper over the page and I asked you to recall the earlier paragraph? For most this will have proved to be quite a difficult exercise because I had employed an information forgetting technique.

It wasn't the paragraph itself that played any part in your forgetfulness but the way in which it was ended. It is all in the five words "It's as simple as that".

Contained in these words are a number of sub-conscious triggers that literally wire straight into the brain and tell it to act in a certain way and in this case to forget all that has gone before.

First of all I want you to consider the phrase "It's as simple". What is it implying? What does it tell your sub-conscious? What is it telling your ego?

The word "simple" implies to anyone you are communicating with that the subject you are talking about is not a difficult one and should be easily understood by anyone with the smallest amount of intelligence. Now think about whom you are likely to be communicating with. Decision makers? Buyers? Husbands? CEO's or Business owners?

The one character trait each of these personalities will have is a sense of pride. It is the conscious act of not wanting to damage their sense of pride that WILL prevent any one of these people from interrupting and questioning you because to interrupt and to question is to admit that your simple solution or concept is something their intellect is not capable of understanding.

Imagine yourself being told by a manager that the concept they are presenting is a simple one. What are the chances of you now interrupting them and confessing that you are not as intelligent as you were given credit for?

$10,000 Key Point: *People with pride will in most cases agree with, or claim understanding of, topics they have no or little understanding of.*

I suppose you must be wondering how do the words "as that" work?

I want to take you back to your childhood when you asked your mother or father for permission to do something they did not want you to do. How did that conversation end?

The chances are that it went something like this: "NO….and that is that".

As a child what is that telling you? With your parents choosing their words carefully, although not consciously, they effectively put an end to all future communication on that subject. Or another way they could have put it is "NO… period!"

So now when we place "it's as simple as that" at the end of a statement it says to the person you are communicating with that what you have just described is a simple concept and you'll accept no questioning as you are moving on.

There is a final part to this technique which improves its effectiveness enormously. Once you have delivered, "it's as simple as that", you must now move on to a different subject immediately. Again, because our brains are so lazy this change of subject will cause your client to forget the previous subject and latch onto the next.

Enough theory, it's about time you had some examples:

Example 1:

You: "Mark, this software integrates via a standard USB interface or through a single CSTA serial bus which makes processor unit integration very flexible and is less of a drain on the LAN... it's as simple as that."

You: "Just out of interest, have you seen how it will all look on screen yet, Mark, because I've got it here if you want to have a look?"

You read through all that theory for such a short example? Yes, I'm sorry but at least you know all the psychological triggers being employed here and as a passing thought... Without looking, what was said before, "It's as simple as that"?
　　Tell me I got you? If so then, how easy was that...it's genius.

Example 2:

You: "Ethan, the best I can offer is a mortgage spread over a 30 year term, which brings the monthly payment down to $1600 at a rate of 4.5% on an interest only loan which I know is $314 more expensive than you were originally looking to spend but I really haven't anywhere else to try, it's as simple as that."

You: "Do you want to see the new photographs of the property with the newly converted cattle barn I got this morning?"

Customer: "Yeah, go on then."

You: "Here you go have a look at these; the builders have done such a great job. Did you say you were thinking of having a pool built next to the barn?"

Looking at both examples they are either communicating a subject that is often quite difficult to understand or a subject that you don't want the customer to dwell on at that stage in your presentation. Both rely on you the salesperson to end the subject with, "it's as simple as that", and then move on to a topic that is more appealing to the brain causing it to delete or forget everything that went immediately before it.
　　Do you recall the details of the mortgage in example 2? What if I were to say $1600?
　　This technique enables you the salesperson to have your customer temporarily forget the details of your presentation. So if your customer wants to know details of pricing or term arrangements then this technique allows you to be honest in telling them but enabling you to move on quickly, address reasons

why your product, service or idea is good for the business and then re-address the topic of price later when he will recall your earlier conversation. Of course the second time the price is addressed the customer will have had you explain various added benefits not mentioned earlier.

How useful to you is that?

If you have anything like my sense of humor then this technique happens to be not only useful but can be really funny if used socially. I can often be found sitting with friends and asking them to comment on a subject I was speaking about. Of course they have no clue because I'd since moved on with the, "it's as simple as that", technique. I may try this three or four times before I pretend to be getting quite annoyed at them for not listening to me. The confusion on their face is brilliant to see and is very funny.

Mind Reading

Ok, I'll admit something to you. The very first line of this chapter was "....I guess you are wondering why I have mis-spelt the word 'focusing'?"

You all know as well as I do that the spelling of "focusing" is actually correct but as a result of me posing the question you more than likely made sure by going over the word again? Isn't it strange that on being told it was wrong, your brain went back, spelled it out and questioned itself even though you knew it was spelled correctly?

What was being used here was a strategy that enables you to instantly change the direction and focus of somebody's thoughts towards whatever it is you want them to think about.

On reading the first line of the chapter did you for one second think that the word "focusing" was spelled wrong? Of course you didn't but as soon as I had told you that, that is exactly what you were wondering (thinking) then it is exactly that which you were thinking about. Even now that I have told you what I have done and how I have done it I wonder how many of you actually did see the mistake in the spelling of "directed"? I suggest very few of you spotted it because not many people look at things with that level of detail.

Not again, this is too easy! Ok, I'll say it again and for the last time. There is no mistake in the spelling of "directed" but hopefully I have proved just how easy and powerful this strategy is.

Thought Changing

As you saw in the last section, because of the laziness of the brain, it is very easy to get someone to temporarily forget what it is we are communicating. It is also true that our brains have little to no attention span when given a new stimulus to think about.

A brief example of this is when you have in your mind a great topic of conversation, a fantastic idea or a nailed on discussion point and then another person asks you a question. I'm sure we've all been there when suddenly it is our turn to speak and our brain literally empties itself of all intelligence and solution thinking and replaces it with BLANK! Why? Because someone or something gave your brain something else to think about and in turn it forgot what you were going to say!

Before we get down to some laser beam examples I'd just like to spend a bit of time showing how this works.

I know what you all must be thinking if you've got this far, I wonder how he got to find this out?

Were you really, I very much doubt it but for most of you I bet you are now and if so then isn't this the perfect time to answer your well thought out question?

Please tell me I didn't get you AGAIN?

$10,000 Key Point: *By telling a customer that you know what he is thinking you will cause him to think exactly that. When suggested that a customer must be wondering about (X) then it is (X) he will now wonder about it. Isn't this just the best thing ever?*

Laser Beam Examples

Example 1:

You: "I suppose you are wondering what the next step is?"
Customer: "Ah… yeah what is the next step?"
(To reply no to this is almost rude enough for them never to say it.)

Example 2:

You: "I know what you must be thinking; it's a lot of property for the asking price?"
Customer: "Well yeah it is."
(To reply no to this is almost rude enough for them never to say it.)

Example 3:

Customer: "We have maintenance covered already."
You: "I suppose you must be wondering what happens in years 2, 3 & 4?)
Customer: "Ok, what happens in 2, 3 & 4?"
(To reply no to this is almost rude enough for them never to say it.)

Example 4:

Customer: "Ummm… it's a little bit more than we were looking to part with."
You: "I guess you must also be thinking about the delivery time."
Customer: "Ok, what is the delivery time?"
You: "It's going to be that it's this one or a ten week waiting list."
(This started as a negotiation over price and ended with one question being an alternative choice.)

Key Point: *The use of mind reading questions causes the person you are communicating with to think exactly what you told them to think.*

Secondary Suggestions

Ever wondered how to get people to do things they wouldn't ordinarily do? What about getting people to do more than they would normally do? What about getting people to be more accepting of your requests?

All three of these questions can and will be answered with the technique of secondary suggestion.

As a rule I don't like to eat cheese. It's not that I am allergic to cheese but more that I just don't like the taste. This throughout my life has been a minor annoyance that has caused me no end of trouble when eating out at a restaurant or ordering a fast food burger.

For years I have had to ask for a "Double Bacon Cheeseburger" without the cheese please and watch the server's face look at me as if I were an alien or the biggest inconvenience known to mankind. I have never really understood why this request was met with "what are you like" type reaction. I simply don't like the taste of cheese.

Anyway, back to the story. As I said I have had to ask for, "No cheese", for as long as I can remember so imagine my delight when by accident I discovered a new way of ordering my food.

It happened when by chance I stumbled across a burger bar that didn't have a "Double Bacon Cheeseburger" on its menu but in its place there were "Hamburger, Cheeseburger and Burger options including Chili sauce, Barbeque sauce and Bacon".

This was now an easy ordering process.

Gary: "Could I have a Hamburger please?"
Assistant: "Certainly, any options with that?"
Gary: "Yes please, could I add bacon?"
Assistant: "Ok, that's one Hamburger with Bacon. Anything else?"

No funny looks, No tutting under their breath, no looking like I was an alien and no "Are you mad?" rolling of the eyes! This was brilliant except for one minor detail. I had never seen another one of these burger places ever before, so this was likely to be my first and last time of getting treated as a burger individualist. (A bit melodramatic I know but…. I DON'T LIKE CHEESE!!!)

This event however got me wondering if all burger ordering in the future could be as easy. The next time I went to a very well known burger establishment I thought I'd try my newfound knowledge. I walked straight up to the assistant who dutifully asked what I wanted and instead of asking for a "Double Bacon Cheeseburger" I simply asked for a basic Double Hamburger. As she was just about to put it through the register I asked casually, "Could you add some bacon to that please?" To my amazement she looked up with a big smile and said "Yes, that's fine sir".

I have tried this out several times in various different places and it always works. It would appear that if you ask for something to be taken away, you get looked at like you're an alien but ask for something to be added as a "Secondary Suggestion" and it's ok!

We have all fallen for this strategy when used by our employers, family and friends. Think about all the times you have gotten up to get your partner something to drink. What happens if, as you are walking to the door your partner asks if you can bring them a sandwich or chocolate bar back with you? Well of course you just fulfill the request without question because you are a nice person. Ok, what if we turned the clock back and you were both sitting watching TV and your partner asks, "Honey, can you go to the kitchen and get me a drink and make me a sandwich please?" Are you so keen to do it now?

Key Point*: Secondary Suggestions work on the premise that you have already committed to a single request. Whilst fulfilling that first request if someone suggests a second or third action then you are FAR more likely to carry out the order.*

Suggestions In The Work Place

I have met so many salespeople, consultants and other persuaders who all need to ask a fairly standard set of questions on the completion of an order.

For example; "I'm going to need a Tax number, Company number, full address, email contact details and bank details to name but a few."

The problem with this is that there are simply too many things required to complete the order and I have been told stories of prospects actually NOT going ahead because it simply sounds too scary. This is where we can use "Secondary Suggestions" to make this process seem easy and less scary.

Example 1:

You: "Kat, all I'm going to need is something with your full address and email contact details on please."

Customer: "Ok, I'll just get those details for you."

(As the customer is taking this action you can now make your "Secondary Suggestion")

You: "Oh, by the way, while you're there could you get your bank and company details for me?"

Customer: "No problem."

To indicate why this works I just want to go back over this last example and re-write it with what is normally said.

Example 1b:

You: "Kat, all I'm going to need is something with your full address and email contact details on, your bank details and also you company registration details."

How scary is that for anyone!

Example 2:

You: "Can you write that in your diary for me Dave for the 27th?"
Customer: "Yes I can do that."
You: "While you're there can you put a note a week before to remind you that you need to call Brynley by the 25th?"

I know what you're thinking. That sounds too obvious. Think about it… Were you actually thinking it's obvious?

I agree it does sound as if you needn't have to bother with something like above until you ask for it all in the same request and notice how your chances of getting EVERYTHING done reduces.

Example 2b:

You: "Can you write that in your diary for me Dave for the 27th and a note for the week before reminding you that you need to call Brynley by the 25th?"

Key Point: This strategy will MAXIMIZE your chances of getting everything you need done without mistakes, without causing annoyances and without causing anguish.

The best way to perfect this is to use it while at home and get your family and friends to do something extra for you without them even knowing.

Better Out Than In!

I'll say it before you do; this has nothing to do with any bodily functions what so ever!

This section is all about the things that many sales people either find the hardest or avoid even mentioning. I am talking about objections, resistance and reasons to say no.

My experience of sales is that there are too many salespeople who will adopt a "fingers crossed" approach to a customer finding out all the gory details of a proposal. I don't subscribe to these methods at all. If you cannot be honest and up front about your product, service or idea, then don't sell it.

In saying that I am all in favor of a salesperson having the skills and aptitude to sell the "down sides" of his or her product with the use of technique and strategy, which is what we will discover below.

Firstly we need to distinguish between what are called Alpha and Omega strategies.

Alpha Strategies are those in which a sales offering is added to in order to increase the chances of getting a YES. *(Giving a discount, bundling additional products, giving referrals.)*

Omega Strategies are those that align a sales offering to reduce the chances of getting a NO.

It is the use of Omega strategies that we will be concentrating on as they are largely under used and not understood by many.

Having trained a great many sales professionals I have come to discover that there are a limited amount of real objections that a customer will have against the purchase of your product, service or idea. What we will be doing in the next two scenarios is understanding how we can minimize their effect and lead you towards the yes response you desire.

You Are Too Expensive

I'm sure you have heard this too many times no matter what it is you are selling in whatever industry. Often this resistance to your price is simply a reaction to trying to get the best deal. The problem you face is that if you now enter into a negotiation over price you can often belittle your product. This is where the statement below will overcome this by pre-empting the question over price BEFORE it ever comes into the conversation.

Scenario: Before you ever ask the customer for his reaction to your price and before they have a chance to comment you say the following:

You: "I'll say it before you do, we are slightly more expensive than many of our competitors but for good reason."

What you will now want to do is explain all of the points that stand your product, service or idea apart from all others. This very simple phrase will literally take away your customer resistance towards your price because you have said the exact thing he was going to object to.

Can your customer now object to you being more expensive? Have you now identified the one thing he was going to say no to? Does this take away his resistance?

Installation Process

The installation process objection is often a hidden one and is not brought up by a customer as a reason for not wanting to go ahead with your proposal. A normal response to this is usually the dreaded but easily overcome 'I want to think about it' (See Role Projection).

If during your presentation you fail to satisfy a customer about your expertise and fail safe methods of installation this will result in a no sell, so it is with an Omega strategy that you can overcome it.

Scenario: (During the course of your product presentation.)

You: "Many customers fear the installation process; as the last thing you want is to experience three days down time. Employees not being able to work due to engineers working overhead and then having to be trained in thirty minutes before they go off site. This is why we have designed our installation process so that this cannot and will not happen....... Does that alleviate any worry you might have had?"

Will the hidden objection of installation now come back? Were you able to put questions in the mind of the customer about your competitors' processes?

What you have just done is what I like to call "Emotional Oscillation". If you can, think of a dial with '-10' at one end '0' in the middle and '+10' at the other. Before you used this strategy there is a good chance that the customer might have been ambivalent towards your offer making him a '0'. By addressing the installation process in terms of fear and making it sound like a living nightmare it is with good judgment you can assume the customer has emotions approaching the '-10' mark and by you putting it right, making him feel secure and letting him see your outcome where he was '0' then '-10' he will now be '+10'. Oscillating his emotions.

Bonus Mind Focusing Techniques

Here is a quick list of other phrases that can be employed to direct your customer's thought toward making a good decision.

1: "I guess this goes without saying…"
(By stating something is/was obvious prevents interruption and creates compliance.)

2: "It's not rocket science is it?"
(Similar effect to 'It's as simple as that'.)

3: "I'll go over this quickly because I'm guessing you'll already know all about it."
(Stops interruptions and pushes the pride button.)

4: "You'll already know we're not the cheapest from the products we sell and our reputation in your marketplace."
(This one works in minimizing the 'price' objection. Firstly you have told him you are not the cheapest and secondly you are assuming that he knows why it is, which stops the negotiation.)

Summary

Selling does not have to be the profession of lies and underhanded methods many have come to think of it as. With intelligence and a high standard of ethics YOU can get a customer to purchase your product, service and ideas because they actually want to buy it.

A building doesn't always need a demolition machine to bring it down. Often a strategic brick will do.

There you go, have fun, use this information ethically at all times - and happy selling!

Chapter Four

Role Projection

Have you ever wondered how your life would have panned out were you to have been given a completely different name? Ever get an opinion of someone before meeting him or her because of the name they were given at birth? Have you ever thought you were not going to get on with someone because you know someone else with the same name and you didn't like him or her?

I imagine the majority of answers to the above, if not all of them would be a resounding, "YES!"

So in that case I'll ask you just one more. Why does a simple name hold so much power of what people think about you?

The answer is *Role Projection.*

Going through our lives we all would like to think that we are individuals, making our own decisions and are intellectually strong enough not to be lead by others. I too would love to believe this about my decisions but unfortunately we do nothing of the sort and in many cases and as we will see, we are simply dancing to the tunes that other people play for us. We are a collection of roles that other people want us to be.

So how can this be, why does it happen and what does it have to do with selling?

Whose Role are you playing?

I'd like to tell you a brief story. The story starts way back when I was at school and around seven years old. It was a glorious sunny day and the grounds man was out riding his tractor cutting the grass on the football field. My teacher, Mr. Wallace, wrote up on the black board a list of ten Math questions for the class to complete with an incentive that once we had completed them and scored full marks we could get changed and play softball outside. With that I wrote out the questions as fast as I could, didn't say a word to anyone, covered up my answers so that no one could copy and was the first person to go up to the front of the class and hand over my work. Mr. Wallace sat there for a while with his red pen in hand and slowly but purposefully went down the page ticking the correct answers as he went. "Ten out of ten", he said in front of the class. "Off you go Gary, go and get changed; you are free to go outside".

I was so happy to be the first to complete my work and felt infinitely proud that the teacher had commented on my brilliance in front of my peers. A truly happy and what I didn't realize at the time life-changing event!

A couple of weeks later a similar task was given to the class except this time it was English Language. The teacher placed a list of ten words on the board and we were asked to write whether the words were nouns, verbs or adjectives. Twenty minutes later I was still getting sent back to my desk, X's next to my wrong answers made by the same red pen I'd loved only two weeks previous. I'd managed to get them completely wrong. I didn't understand the exercise and to my disgust and embarrassment my peers were looking through the window laughing and waiting for me so that they could play softball.

This story will be the same as many others about school but it is a story that has shaped the rest of my life and similar stories will have shaped yours.

In those two afternoons it was confirmed to me that I was talented at Math while I wasn't so good at English. This is where Role Projection starts for many of us. We are told by parents and teachers that we are better at some things and not so good at others.

So what happened from that day forward that has changed my life? Well, it is only human nature to want praise and adulation for doing something that is recognized as being good. It is ingrained in our psyche to try to please others whether it is our parents, our children or even our employer just so that one day they will thank us for what we have done. In my case from that very moment in the Math class I looked forward to the days in which the teacher wrote up Math questions on the board because I knew that if only I could finish first and get all the answers correct that I would again be singled out in front of the class and praised for the work I had produced. I really don't think that my teacher or in fact any teacher realizes just how much we their pupils are influenced by the public showing of praise or criticism from them as mentors and how it can affect us in such a deep and lasting way.

The same is also true but in reverse for those horrible English problems. I dreaded them. I didn't want to be last to complete them. I didn't want everyone else to know that I didn't know the answers but because of the way in which I was made to feel foolish I didn't feel there was any point in trying to improve as many had come to their conclusions which confirmed to me that I simply wasn't gifted in that subject.

I wonder what would have happened if I had unknowingly and without real knowledge of what I was doing got 10 out of 10 for those English questions. How much would it have changed my outlook if I'd been praised in front of the class as producing good work? Well I do know that I would have definitely wanted to hear the praise again and maybe with that self-belief have tried all the harder to get it and thereafter become a better English student.

Even today, I consider my strength to be Math and not English and it is all down to the Role that one teacher gave me when I was seven years old. Does he know what an influence he has had on me? Does he know how much I wanted to live up to his expectations of me? Does he know how he shaped my academic life towards Math and praise and away from English and ridicule? Probably not!

I want you to take a couple of minutes and think about what roles you have been given throughout the course of your life. Has anyone told you that you are talented at a particular thing and not so good in another? Who was it that said you were not very good at sports? When did someone praise you for your talents? Have you ever been told you are better at selling to one type of person than another? Or told you that you are suited to sell to one sort of industry more than others?

Let's face it, why would you bother to work really hard at something when realistically you were guaranteed not to get any sort of praise for it? Isn't it easier to try harder with something you are told you're good at and get recognized for the results?

Key Question: *Is it possible to tell someone that they have good characteristics even though they don't? Would they then play the role of the good person you just told them they were?*

It's All In The Name

I asked at the very start of the chapter whether you had ever given any consideration to what your life would be like if you were given a different name.

Would your friends still want to be your friends? Would people still be interested in and respect what you say? Would you have the same interests? Would your life have followed the same path?

Once you have answered the questions above I have one final consideration for you and I would like you to really think about the answer that you come up with. Give it plenty of thought because the implications of your answer might be huge!

What has attracted your life to you? Was it your hard work and intellect or was it simply people liking your name?

Key Question: *Can you influence someone simply by using their name and attaching a set of values to that name?*

Respect Or Not?

As we have just seen, the name of someone can have an enormous effect on how we view that person simply because of the set of values we attribute to their name. The same can be true for somebody's job role or job title.

Let's take the position of Salesperson.

All those years ago did you ever think to yourself or tell anyone that you were going to be a Salesperson? For most of us this would be a definite no. There are not many who aspire to become a Salesperson when they leave school but rather fall into a sales role after giving something else a go for a period of time.

So why then do not many people say when they leave school, "I want to be a Salesperson"?

Maybe one answer is that the career of a professional Salesperson is not often spoken about by teachers or career advisors, who would rather give advice to pupils about heading towards careers in the Military, Engineering, Legal Profession or Medicine. Thinking back I cannot ever remember being given any career advice or direction and hearing the word Sales in any conversation.

Why then is the role of Salesperson not something many children grow up desperately wanting to be or not a profession often spoke about by those in a position of career development?

Are there any connotations that come with the job role Salesperson? What does the word Salesperson mean to the general public? What does the role say about you, your personality or your grades in school?

Again, years of people attributing all salespeople with a set of standard ethics and values has meant that many people believe we are a certain type of character just because of the name of our profession. Fair? I don't think so.

These then are the reasons why we don't come out of school applying for every sales position going nor do we want to tell everyone we meet about being a Salesperson.

Role Projection has played a huge part in enabling others to act on previous knowledge and experience, bring them into the present and attribute those very same characteristics to you the 'Salesperson'. You are now 'just like' all the sales people who have gone before you, attributed with the same mentality, the same motives to sell and the same set of ethics.

Respected Or Not?

Let's now look at one more example on how Role Projection plays a part in our every day communications before we get down to the discovery of real life uses and applications and the Salesperson's holy grail, how to overcome the eternal objection, "I want to think about it".

Many of you will be selling your product, ideas or services while meeting all types of people from all walks of life. It has been said in so many books and by so many sales managers and trainers that you should not pre-judge an appointment before you go in and meet with the person. That said, how easy is it to rid your conscious thoughts of past experiences selling to people in that industry? How easy is it to not pre-judge an individual by looking at their name and relating that to someone else you know who shares it? The answer to this is pretty near impossible.

Can it be possible to stop yourself from thinking?

Scenario:

You have just checked your diary on Monday morning, you have an appointment booked to see the CEO of a mid-ranged company tomorrow whose name is Bill Clinton. Stop. Pause.

What are you first thoughts? How old is he? What color hair does he have? How tall is he? How does he sound? What is his wife's name?

As soon as you read the CEO's name a whole character came into your conscious thoughts, his personality, his appearance and whether you'd even like the guy. It is from these thoughts that you made and will make your pre-judgments.

What then is likely to happen tomorrow when you turn up and meet with this person? Firstly you might meet the guy and say, "You look nothing like what I was expecting" or, "You really do look like Bill Clinton". Now how can you say any of these statements without pre-judging the appointment or person? You can't. The reason is that Role Projection has already been at work.

Role Projection gave you a feeling, a set of characteristics and tempted you to predict what that person would be like.

Role Giving

Earlier I asked two Key Questions about the use of Role Projection.

Key Question: Is it possible to tell someone they have good characteristics even though they don't? Would they then play the role of the good person you just told them they were?

Key Question: Can you influence someone simply by using their name and attaching that name with a set of values?

In this section you will be discovering how, when and why to use Role Projection to aid you in influencing your outcome. The information in the section is VERY powerful and can get you what you want, when you want it. Use it wisely!

Does she mean it or not?

You meet a beautiful woman at a bar and offer her a drink. You spend the next couple of hours talking, buying drinks and having a really good evening. As a parting comment you suggest that the two of you should meet up for dinner on the following Saturday evening at your favorite romantic restaurant, to which she agrees.

10 o'clock Saturday night. The meal was delicious, the wine was magnificent and the company was perfect. The woman leans over and whispers these beautiful words.... "Can I tell you something?" she says. "The thing I like about you most is that you are such a great listener. I feel like I could tell you anything and you'd just listen and take it all in. Do you fancy meeting again on Wednesday evening?"

"YES! YES! YES!" you say in a calm and unsurprised manor.

Well ok, I know that doesn't happen to people who look like you and I but it's a nice story with a happy ending and so we'll just have to run with it.

Exercise:

Write down what role you believe is going to be played out by you the next time you meet this woman. How did the woman get you to play this role, what words did she use and how would she feel should you not play the role?

Analysis:

The woman in question has been a master at giving you a role to play in preparation for your next date. She has taken the act of listening, attributed it as being a good thing and then placed that role onto you.

Even though you might know you are the world's worst listener and no one has ever said anything like this before, what are you going to ensure you do more than anything else when you next meet this woman on Wednesday night? That's right, you are going to listen to what ever she tells you all night long. The reasons for this are two fold. First, you will be desperate not to offend her and prove her previous judgment wrong of you and secondly you will want to hear her praise you again for having this vital skill. Oh and there is a third but that's for the following Saturday night which we don't have time for!

Key Point: The act of telling someone they are good at something will cause them to want to play out your projections.

Role Reciprocity

Your life insurance policy has ended and you want to get a good price from your insurance company. How do you get the agent to give you a good price?

"Hello, ABC insurance how can I direct your call?"
"Hi I'm looking to renew my life insurance policy."
"Ok I'll just connect you to that department."

"Good Morning, Gary speaking how can I help?"
"Ah hello Gary I thought I recognized the name, I think it was you who was such a help last time. You're about the only person who I spoke to who didn't use insurance jargon or over inflate the price. How are you?"

Exercise:

What role have you just placed onto poor, unsuspecting Gary? How have you influenced Gary to get you what you are after? How does he feel about you and what is he now looking to provide and ensure?

Analysis:

You have told him he was really helpful last time, you remembered him from your last conversation, you appreciated his lack of jargon and that he gave you an honest price. More importantly you have praised him for these attributes and values.

Gary will now feel dutiful to play out the role of a helpful and friendly person, will stay clear of complicated legal jargon and won't over inflate the price because he will not want you to change your opinion of him because he likes the praise and the fact you like him. For him now to give you an over inflated price and not give you what you are after, he runs the risk of you changing your opinion of him and the company he works for. This in itself is a very important point worth noting. Which is more likely to hurt his self-esteem and morale, your opinion of him or your opinion of the company?

Did your previous call with Gary ever happen? Are you doing any harm? No, you are simply making someone feel good about himself to help you get what you want without paying too much for it.

Key Point: In many cases when placed in this type of situation a person will almost certainly think about how they are portrayed more so than how their employer is perceived. Humans need to feel that they are appreciated and liked by other humans and so company loyalty will often be put aside to gain the praise of another.

Have you ever had cause to call a customer service line to complain? Have the company agents ever apologized for the way their company acts? Did they suggest they would do something for you that wasn't normal company policy?

Generally people will not want to disappoint another who has already expressed that they like them for being a certain way.

Give Them The POWER!

You have a meeting with a CEO of medium sized company. You arrive 30 minutes early, you feel good that you have researched the company, you look smart and you are ready to go in.

The CEO greets you and takes you up to the boardroom where he offers you a seat and asks you what it is you are there for. The next 5 minutes are spent explaining to him why you are there, what it is that your company does and how this can improve his business in the future. You then ask this simple yet effective question.

"Gary, just out of interest, are you the main decision maker?"
"Yes the decisions stop with me", he says, sitting upright and proud in his comfy leather chair.
"Great, the reason I ask is that as you'll know there is nothing worse than getting to the end of a presentation only to be told there are another 3 people to get Yes's from", you say sitting uncomfortably on a small plastic red chair that was brought in from the canteen!

Exercise:

How will he now feel if he has to say, *"I have a board of Directors I need to run this past?"*

Analysis:

This really does work and I have proved it over and over again. You have just given this CEO a role to play that he'll want to live up to or else look stupid in front of you.

By using Role Projection you have given him the power to make a decision, inflated his position and expressed how frustrating it is to have other CEO's in his position NOT make a decision.

Key Point: *Role Projection can give people a perceived power to do things because if then they do not live up to the role then they are at risk of being found out or looking stupid.*

Are We Really Who We Say We Are?

The idea of role projection and how it can be used has fascinated me for many years because as an individual I truly believed that I had made my own decisions with my own values and my own goals independent from others' influences. So are we really living the independent life we all believe we do or are we just an amalgamation of many roles being asked of us? Can we really watch TV and be immune from advertising role projections and can we really be ourselves with family, friends and colleagues if we are constantly striving for the praise of others playing the roles they have given us to play?

Ideas and Applications

In this section I would like to give you some brief but very specific ideas and applications on how easy it is to use Role Projection to sell to virtually anyone and in every situation. Please use this section to find ways of utilizing this superb influencing tool to your benefit when thinking about your product, service or idea.

Ideas for different sales areas:

Real Estate: "I'm so pleased I am taking you around this next property because having already got some ideas from you I know the two of you will instantly walk in and see the true potential of this house especially when you can picture your life and belongings in each room."

Role Projection: You have indicated to this couple that you are pleased and honored to have the privilege of showing them around the property and therefore they will not want to let you down. Secondly you have given them a special characteristic standing them out from others, which is to be able to see past existing décor and the ability to imagine their life in the house.

Now this is where you have to keep a straight face because when this works it is really quite hard not to smile too much. As this couple walks through the door of the property listen to the words that they start to use. "I can see the potential." "Wouldn't our sofa look nice there?" "If you take away the furniture and the color of the walls then…" Coincidence?

Car Salesman: "Ok, I have the exact car for you. It's so refreshing to meet someone who understands what they want. There is nothing worse than people who go around kicking tires and bartering on price only to waste everyone's time."

Role Projection: First, you like and have praised the person in front of you for knowing what he wants. In reality he may not have even known what he wanted but because you've given a good characteristic he now follows and wants to appeal to your kind words. Secondly you have shown a dislike for time wasters and price bartering IF they have no thought of doing business.

Direct Sales: "Thanks for your time today. You wouldn't believe how many people we call who say they have no interest in improving business and maximizing current expenditure. It always amazes me."

Role Projection: The characteristics you have just given this person are the complete opposite of the person they will now want to be and play out for you. From this one statement you will hear phrases such as, "We're always looking to improve business." Really? "We are definitely not like that." And, "If we can maximize our expenditure we're always willing to listen."

The list of applications are endless and are worthy of a book in their own right but before we get down to overcoming the salesperson's nemesis I would like to show you how this strategy can be used if you are the consumer.

Buying a business suit: "Hello there, is there something specific you are looking for?" you are asked. Acting surprised you say "Ah thank you. I have just been to one of your competitors who were so unhelpful I had to walk out in the end. They didn't seem to care what I was looking for."

Role Projection: All you need to do now is sit back, relax and enjoy your new personal shopper. I can personally recommend this strategy as I use it where ever I go and whatever I am buying. Due to you pointing out how disappointed and frustrated you were at the way their competitors treated you, this will ensure they will not want to emulate your previous experiences and over compensate by bowing to your every need. Superb!

STOP THE PRESSES!!!

'I Want To Think About It' Overcome!

This is the jewel in the crown when it comes to using Role Projection as a sales person. Being a salesperson myself I know from experience how disheartening, frustrating, disappointing and annoying it is having done a fantastic presentation, worked really hard on getting the right price and found real tangible benefits for the customer, for them to turn to you and utter the dreaded six words. "I want to think about it."

It was after hearing this too many times and overcoming it less times than I wanted that I decided to develop a strategy using Role Projection to get the customer not to say it in the first place.

I am going to spend a few moments asking you to consider three questions and setting a scene where you can use Role Projection to its maximum effect.

1: If a friend of yours told you that the action you just did made you look stupid, would you be inclined to do it again?

2: If you saw someone else doing an action that made them look stupid would that put you off doing the same action?

I think in both cases most of us would agree that if something makes you look stupid or is embarrassing then the chances of doing that action or repeating it are greatly reduced. This then is a strategy that we are going to employ to reduce the chances of a customer saying, "I want to think about it".

3: Have you ever been in a dispute or argument with someone where they tell you exactly what you are just about to do? For example:

"Then I suppose you are going out to the bar now?"

What happens when you hear these words? Our teenage years and actions come flooding back and most will rebel at being told what they are going to do with an action to defy the assumption. In the above most people will then do ANYTHING rather than go to the bar and prove the person who said it right.

The same is true for, "I want to think about it". We will be telling the customer this is exactly what they are going to say and implying that they would look stupid in doing so and will in most cases ensure that they do something completely different to save face.

The Scene: The situation is that you need to convince the person sitting in front of you (not literally as we discovered in an earlier chapter) to commit to buying your product, taking on your idea or using your service.

You have done a great opening pitch, you've set out your agenda and things are going as planned. After asking your probing fact finding questions you have in mind the ideal solution which you are just about to present.

The presentation went really well and you got some good buying signals from the customer with the nodding of the head, the leaning forward and the positive responses to your trial closing questions. This then sounds like it's all moving in the right direction, however how many times have you thought that, only to hear the "think about it" line?

So here we go.... Sit back, relax and welcome to my secret, which I have kept to myself for years but am just about to share with all! This has NEVER been written about before and certainly never been taught. This IS my "Holy Grail".

While doing a great presentation I am going to ask you to say and DO the following:

1: Ask the customer, "Are you happy with everything we have gone through so far?" *(You already know the answer to this as you have seen the buying signals throughout.)*

2: "Have you got any questions or are you happy for me to move on?" *(If at this stage the customer has any questions then it is NOW that you MUST answer them or else the final and most impressive part will not work.)*

3: "Great because I'm sure it's the same for your industry, there is nothing worse for me to get to the end and hearing, 'I want to think about it'."
(On delivering, "I want to think about it", you need to perform a "Jazz Hands" gesture. Jazz hands are when you have your hands just outside of shoulder width; splay your fingers out wide and shake those hands!!! Come on don't be embarrassed really shake those hands!!!)

4: Make sure your have a smile on your face and say it in a joking / silly manner or else it will not work as well.

Phew! There it is, out in the open and to my knowledge the best way of overcoming the most difficult and annoying objection known to a salesperson.

Why It Works:

1: You have asked the customer whether he is ok with how the meeting is going.

2: They agree and see that this pleases you because you in return give a nice happy smile.

3: You have asked for permission to proceed and offered an opportunity to ask any questions before moving on.

4: "I'm sure it's the same in your industry" lets the customer know that he doesn't like to hear the excuse of "I want to think about it" in his line of work.

5: "There is nothing worse" tells the customer straight out that if he dares utter those words you will not be very happy and is in complete contrast how you feel about him in point 2.

6: The action of "Jazz Hands" and saying the words, "I want to think about it" in a silly voice is the most powerful use of Role Projection so far. You have just made yourself look quite stupid in front of your customer and maybe you've even embarrassed HIM slightly but by doing so the role will have been taken on board.

7: Internally your customer now knows on every level how the words "I want to think about it" will be received. He knows you will be unhappy, that you know it is just an excuse and best of all that if he says the words he will be perceived as being stupid and embarrassing because you have shown him how everyone else you have heard it from has looked!

8: By you saying, "I want to think about it" and letting him know this is exactly what he would have said will cause the customer to do something completely different in return.

As a salesperson myself I have seen this work so many times and to such great effect. You literally can see their biggest objection and trump card being taken away from them.

How easy was that! I absolutely love this technique; it makes me smile every time I use it. Now you can enjoy the look of "Darn I can't use that now", which I have enjoyed and which has entertained me for years.

Be careful though as like the example earlier you will have to control your joy and happiness when you pull this off. In my experience this simple technique of Role Projection has been the single most profitable tool I have employed both in sales and as a consumer.

Final Thoughts:

We have discovered throughout this chapter how a simple name influences what we think of people we haven't yet met, how they make a judgment on who and what we stand for and even whether we would do business with them. To put this in context and to indicate how powerful this can be, I would like you to consider whether a gentleman called "Barry Humberston–Smyth" would fit into your organization and what role would he likely have? An interesting thought?

As a salesperson we now know how to get customers to play a certain and predetermined role and as consumers how we can manipulate the salesperson.

In the final section you have placed a role for a customer to play, used actions to show how they would look if they don't follow the role and instigated the "teenager" reaction of rebelling to get your desired result.

I will finish the chapter with a question that has in part already been asked.

"Does the life you have come down to your intellect and hard work, or the name you were given at birth and your desire to play a role to please others?"

Good luck, keep this our little secret and say goodbye to "I want to think about it"!

Chapter Five

The Single Most Important Factor In Selling?

....Certainly the Most Underdeveloped Skill

[Ed. Note- Eliot Hoppe, Salesman and Sales Manager has added successful Consultant and in-demand Trainer to his endeavors. Better? He's an awesome person! K.H.]

The main objective of meeting with your customer is ultimately to get them to become a user. For them to trust you and like you, you have to demonstrate credibility, knowledge, resourcefulness, passion and a willingness to learn about them and their business. To be successful, you must be curious, you must ask questions.

Often there seems to be reluctance by many sales reps to drill down into core issues, uncover details about the customer's business, their processes and areas for improvement. In many sales organizations, there is a great deal of urgency and training placed on the sales process and product knowledge. This is very important, yet many organizations overlook investing in the skill of asking great questions, understanding the strategy behind which questions to ask and when to ask them. Asking great questions significantly reduces wasted effort and increases rep yield.

This chapter begins with a personal challenge from me to you.

Before you go any further in this book, I would like you to stop reading after this paragraph. I would like you to close this book, get a pen and paper and write down every single question that you currently ask your customer. This is an investment of your time right now. I want you to write every question down exactly as you ask it, word for word. Take your time. To fully appreciate the benefits of effective questioning, this exercise will prove most valuable. Do it now. Close the book and write down every question. Once you're done, continue reading on.

Imagine this. You have just finished a first appointment sales call with a potential customer. The meeting has ended and you both stand up and reach over the desk and conclude the meeting with a handshake. You leave the customer's office together and begin the walk to the main lobby area where the formal "hand off" occurs. In a final farewell, you look the customer in the eyes, smile, say thank you and shake hands one final time. You both go your separate way. Your customer walks back to their office and you towards your car. You begin to evaluate the sales call in your head and contemplate the next sequence of steps that you have committed to.

There's a small problem however. This call was different. You're now sitting in your car and saying to yourself, "this probably won't lead to anything". Something just didn't feel right. You didn't get the answers you were looking for and you are not sure if you truly connected with the customer. You question if the customer is truly interested or possibly playing two ends to the middle. As for next steps, you did secure a second appointment, which is great, however now you question the true opportunity to have this customer become a user of your product or service. Will you be wasting your valuable time preparing for this next meeting? How much effort will you put into the next call?

Asking great questions eliminates all of the post sales doubt and clearly identifies customer motives, true opportunity and probability to use. Asking great questions will get your customer talking in short stories. This is great because we all like stories. As children we loved to hear a good story. As adults, we continue to converse in short stories. Think about your everyday life. How many conversations do you have every day, which involve a story? Let's begin with, "Good morning, how was the game last night?"

Great questions will:

- ➢ Challenge the status quo (your true competition.)
- ➢ Build trust, confidence, credibility.
- ➢ Lay the relationship foundation for the future.
- ➢ Make you the subject matter expert and "go to" person.
- ➢ Create an impending moment, next step, joint solution.
- ➢ Generate an "aha" moment, a reason to continue or change.
- ➢ Challenge the competition, current internal process, corporate habits.
- ➢ Uncover a buying process, timing, budgets, finances.
- ➢ Ensure you are dealing with the decision maker.
- ➢ Block out your competitors and get you into new opportunities.
- ➢ Uncover industry trends, other opportunities, question their competitors.
- ➢ Address their customer service issues that become your customer service issues.

To be successful in sales, your customer must talk. Great answers are usually relayed in the form of a story. You have to receive and tell great stories that "color in" the picture that begins in black and white. Our stories have to have substance and feeling. They have to create a visual picture of how the world will look with you in the picture.

Self Talk

During the sales call, two things happen. You and your customer talk and think throughout the conversation. Because of this, it's crucial to understand a few basics in human psychology beginning with understanding our customer's capacity to process information and verbalize information. Studies have shown that the average person has the capability to think approximately 400 - 450 words per minute. The average person has the capability of speaking only 100 - 150 words per minute. That leaves approximately 300 words per minute that requires attention and management by the sales professional. Your customer is constantly evaluating you for trust, knowledge, passion, credibility and likeability among a few things. Your job is to keep that self-chatter down to a minimum.

When you have your customer engaged in your presentation and they are speaking or intently listening to you, their self-talk is very low. This is good. When you are interested in something that has your attention, your self-chatter is low. Great questions get your customer to think – that's what you want. But you want the thinking to be objective, positive, reinforcing and confirming.

If your customer is not engaged with you throughout the sales meeting and you find yourself doing most of the talking or simply don't have a captive audience, the customer's self chatter will be at an all time high. This usually happens when you are not demonstrating that this call is of value to the customer. And if you don't bring distinct value to the customer, you will be judged poorly on the customer's likeability scorecard and you will not be perceived as being a subject matter expert.

Realizing that people buy from people, they judge your likeability. Realizing that people purchase with emotion and justify their decision with logic, your customer will judge both you and their decision to use you.

Types of Questions

When you are looking to uncover areas to explore within a customer's account, you have to be specific in the answer that you receive. How you ask the question determines how they will answer. This means that if your question is very "shallow" in nature, so will be the answer. If your question is mind provoking then you will get details in your answer. It's these details that set up the context for you to position your product, service or offering.

To fully understand the different types of questions that you should be asking, you need to think holistically and ask questions accordingly. Once you uncover areas that you would like to explore further, that's when you can do a "deep dive" with additional questions that uncover the root of the issues and the influences of those issues.

Warm – Up Questions

It is imperative that the person who booked the meeting begins the sales call. After a few short pleasantries, you need to begin the meeting. As a rule of thumb, you want to begin with dialogue unrelated to selling. This is a great opportunity to get to know your customer especially during the first meeting. Here is one of the best introductions that I know which I used for years on my first appointments. Every appointment began the same way.

Example:

Sales Rep: "Mr. Smith, before we begin our meeting, is there any value in telling you a little bit about myself and my company first?"
(You must always remember to end it with the word "first" because if they respond with "Yes", it implies to the customer that you will have permission to ask the customer about them and their business – second)

This is a great technique because if their response is "No", you can simply say, "That's fine Mr. Smith, where would you like to begin?"

If they say, "Yes, please go ahead", then proceed with your thirty second commercial (which is addressed in greater detail in Activity Management) and at the end of the commercial say, "So, how about you Mr. Smith. How long ago did you get here and what is it that you do?"

Remember, people love to talk about themselves. After all, it is the single topic that they know best. Be genuine and sincere, it goes far.

Personal Questions

Personal questions are usually asked at the beginning of the sales call. This is to establish commonality between you and your customer. It is a great way to gain valuable insight into the customer's hobbies and interests. These conversations should not include controversial topics that could draw a negative impression of you. You need to be careful of questions that border on strong beliefs and values such as religion, politics and abortion. Not agreeing with a customer on such a point could contaminate the opportunity for the customer to become a user.

Personal questions are great for calibrating body language signals of your customer. Typically the customer is talking about themselves and not business. This allows you to pay close attention to head, body and foot movements while they are in a relaxed state of mind.

Examples:

You: "So Joe, what do you like to do for fun when you aren't here working a 12 hour day?"

You: "I noticed that you have a lot of golf memorabilia. I was wondering, are you an avid golfer or collector?"

You: "If you were to look back on your wonderful career, what accomplishment would you consider your best?"

Competition Questions (Your Customer)

Competition questions, which probe into your customer's competition, will provide many answers. They will reveal to you where they are in the marketplace, who they consider their competitors, what strategies to market they may be considering or implementing, and what values are dear to them which separate their business from the competition. Naturally, this information is invaluable to you as you prepare to present.

Examples:

You: "What strategies have you been able to implement to maintain such a stronghold in market share?"

You: "You mentioned that you are currently the third largest distributor. Strategically, are you planning to increase your position in the future?"

Competition Questions (Status Quo)

These questions probe into the status quo (your true competition) and reveal what you are up against, how they are currently serviced, what they like and what they would like to see improved. You want to uncover all the details, both large and small. This information is invaluable because you will understand what you need to do differently to create distinct value that your competitor currently is not meeting. In addition, your customer will also tell you what you must do to maintain the desired level of service that they are receiving today.

Examples:

You: "You mentioned service is extremely important to you. What is your current supplier doing that you really like? In what areas could they improve?"

You: "When you chose your current supplier, what was the single most important criteria that they had to exceed in order to earn your business?"

Customer Service Questions

Asking your customer about their service levels is a great strategy. Your customer will share with you what service levels they provide their customers, how they measure themselves, what processes are in place and what metrics are important to them. Once you have a clear picture of what is important to your client from a customer service perspective, you will know exactly what metrics you must exceed to change the status quo.

Examples:

You: "You mentioned that your customer service department is measured on how quickly they respond to each inquiry. Just so that I am clear, why is that metric so important to you?"

You: "If I were to ask you to evaluate your current supplier, would it be a perfect 10 on a score card?"
If they say yes, respond with, "That's terrific! Specifically, what is it that they are doing so well?"

More often than not, they will say, "No", at which point you will respond with, "What would your current supplier have to demonstrate to get that perfect score?"

Finance Questions

Most organizations allocate money to fund specific projects and initiatives throughout the year. The question is whether there is a budget to fund or support your product, service or offer. You want to be assured that there are funds available to finance your project. You also want to know if your customer is the decision maker or do they have to go elsewhere for approval. If your customer doesn't have money in the budget to fund the project, are they willing to go and get the funds elsewhere internally?

Examples:

You: "Is there any one department that distributes project funds for the corporation or is each division responsible for their own budget?"

You: "You mentioned that this initiative was implemented late last year. Were you able to submit a budget for the project in time?"

Past Questions

When asking great questions, you have to take the customer back down memory lane. This will establish two benefits to you. For the most part, they will tell you a historical story of how things have evolved - habits, motives and trends within the organization. Quite often, how they did something in the past may tell you a story of how things may move forward with your solution. Past questions will also shed some light on internal processes of who has been involved in the decision making process. This will tell you what's changed and who is involved now, including if your customer is involved in the new process.

Examples:

You: "What would you say are the differences over the last five years that you have noticed with respect to the industry and specifically the way the company has benefited by utilizing technology and other electronic tools?"

You: "You mentioned that two years ago, your company handled those inquiries internally. Now you are outsourcing those same services. What's changed?"

Present Questions

You would be surprised as to how many customers want to live in, and talk about, the present. This is because if there is a problem that they are trying to overcome, it is usually current and the urgency is immediate with expectancy for immediate results. The problem here lies in the fact that people are most comfortable in this area as well.

Examples:

You: "Which training programs are you currently developing for the personal development of your sales teams?"

You: "Since you have implemented the system, what's working well? What areas of improvement would you like to see?"

Future Questions

Future based questioning allows you to uncover company strategies. Is your customer in a growth mode or a downsizing mode? Are they geared to acquire other businesses or are they on the block to be acquired? Are they investing in certain initiatives or cutting back on others?

Future questions will also give you insight into the corporate priorities. It's the answers to these questions that you will want to include in your final presentation. By doing so, your presentation compliments the direction of the customer's future strategic plan and corporate vision.

Examples:

You: "Moving forward, what organizational changes in operations do you foresee in the next 24 months?"

You: "Changes are inevitable in the business world. As you consider changing systems, what requirements must be included to meet your needs for the next 36 months?"

The 5 "W" Questions

Who, What, Where and When questions are necessary in the questioning process because they uncover a multitude of areas to explore within an account. They let you know the participants involved in the decision making process. They also let you receive feedback as to strategies, benefits, directives and timelines. Overall importance in scope and the priority on behalf of the customer are also unlocked by these questions.

"Why" is the single most powerful word in the questioning process. This word unlocks the motives that the customer has and reveals the influences behind the customer's needs. This question also makes the customer think and confirm as to the next action steps that they should take. Correctly used, this question will often compel customers to action.

In addition, these questions will get the customer talking in stories. The skill is to not overuse these "w" questions one after another.

Examples:

You: "Who in your organization was responsible for implementing the current system five years ago?"

You: "What was the primary reason that you implemented the current system?"

You: "Where, internally, within the organization, was the need for more resources uncovered?"

You: "When are the current contracts up for renewal?"

You: "Why did you decide to proceed with that new telephone system?"

Drill - Down Questions

Once you have established that there is a definite area of opportunity that should be explored even further, you require yet a second type of question. Using the "w" questions alone repeatedly could make your customer feel uncomfortable, especially if this is a first meeting. You run the risk of being perceived as an interrogator versus a consultant. Therefore, you want to slightly change up the prefix on the next question. Along with softening the second question, the prefix will direct the customer as to what you are asking them to do. It's the same question, just a different pre-fix.

Examples:

Customer: "Since we acquired the second division last year, our overhead has skyrocketed through the roof and as a result, we are looking to cut costs any way we can."

Sales Expert: "Can you help me understand, what caused the increase in overhead expenses since the acquisition?"

Additional pre-fixes are:

Can you share with me...
Would you elaborate...
Can you help me understand...
In your opinion...
If you could...
Just so that I am clear, does this mean...

Core Issue Questions

Once you have asked the "w" questions and have identified that you would like to explore the opportunity further, you drill down with an additional question.

Based on the response from your customer, you may wish to drill down to a second level. Don't forget that the solution should come from the customer and not you. You now have to get the customer to believe that the solution is theirs and not yours. Lawyers do this in the courtroom and it's called "leading the witness".

The effect is simple and requires you to pay strict attention to one key word in the customer's answer.

Example:

Customer: "…and since then, we made a few changes internally and expected immediate results which up until now, we have not received from both of our departments."

Core Issue Question: "That's interesting. You mentioned immediate results. Specifically, what results were you expecting to get?"

This gets to the core issues and makes your customer think, relive and re-evaluate the past decision and current situation. You must agree with interest, repeat the key word and ask the customer a specific question.

Once you have a customer at this stage, you must resist the urge to talk about your product, service or offering. Sales Experts make note of the core issue and move on to the next question even if they "know" that they can help the customer overcome the issue. Leave nuggets of information for the customer to ponder but leave your aces for your formal presentation.

Questioning Protocol

When asking effective questions, you will be getting great answers. You have to ensure that your curiosity is evident and that you are engaged. The simplest way of conveying that you are engaged when an issue arises is to repeat the stated concern that the customer has raised. Then generate a little anxiety and question the status quo. Your customer should come up with the solution with a little help from you. In the end, your customer should envision the solution with you in it.

Here is a simple questioning process that I want you to remember. It works well when a customer's concern or objection is raised. It assists in uncovering your customer's needs and begins to make both you and your customer think of possible solutions. After all, coming up with a joint solution is what creates the buying environment that you are looking to achieve.

Here is a simple, yet effective, acronym for you to learn: **P.R.O.B.E.**

P – (Problem)

Here is where your listening skills pay off. Remember that your customer will either tell you outright of an issue or concern, or it may be a subtle nuance. In any event you must listen for the problem to see where you may be of benefit. Listening for an area of concern, pain point, challenge or opportunity within the account initiates the PROBE process.

R – (Repeat)

Once you hear a concern or issue that you would like to probe further, you need to repeat the stated issue. This ensures that the customer understands that you are listening. It also allows you to confirm with the customer if this is an area to probe further (together).

O – (Outcome – Desired)

This next step allows you to zero in on a concern that you would like to explore further. All that needs to be done here is to pass the ball back into the customer's court in the form of a question, which asks them what would be the desired outcome that they are looking for. This is the first stage where the customer begins to visualize the perfect outcome.

B – (Bring yourself and your company into the picture)

Now you should be armed with enough knowledge to begin to understand where you and your company fit in. It is critical at this point to resist the urge to talk about everything that your product and service can provide. By talking about you, the focus of the sales call switches from the customer to yourself.

You must remain focused on the need that your customer has expressed. The skill is to leave a hint that you have a possible solution. A great method is to ask a question that would provide a "yes" response.

E – (Emotion and Empathy)

Here is where you have the opportunity to pique interest and create that impending moment that your customer must continue the dialogue with you.

Demonstrate interest and empathy. Be genuine and attentive. Leave the impression that you have an answer. If necessary, leave bits of information and move onto the next question. This maintains the momentum of the questioning process.

Summarize in more detail when all of your pain points have been collected.

At this stage, the issue will be a point of concern (pain point) that both of you have identified. This will most certainly become a point that you will solve and as such, will be included in your final proposal or presentation.

P.R.O.B.E. Questioning Process Example

Below is an example of how this very simple, yet effective, process can work. Here is a dialogue between a sales training company representative and the V.P. of Sales.

VP: "Our sales team nationally is doing well. We have a great group of sales professionals and managers. I am very pleased with our performance last year and our budgets for this year have increased significantly. We need to invest in developing everyone's sales skills further. We firmly believe in investing in our business and people."

Training Expert: "So that I am clear, you had a very successful year and your budgets have been raised significantly for this year. As a result, you would like to invest in the personal development of your sales team. Is that correct?"

VP: "Yes"

Training Expert: "Specifically, what skills or areas of development are you considering for your team?"

VP: "Our sales managers were proactive and recently polled our sales team members and asked the entire team what areas in sales training or development they would like to receive this year. The feedback was positive towards training. Our sales team members stated that they wanted to make more sales and exceed the new budgets for this year. There is concern about having the time to make more sales presentations. They already conduct fifteen sales presentations a week. They figure that if they could make more presentations, they would make more sales. The consensus is that they want to sell more this year and make more money."

Training Expert: "If it were possible, what would be the benefit to your sales team if they were able to increase sales without necessarily having to increase the number of sales calls that they had to book?"

VP: "This would be very beneficial. Our sales team members already visit fifteen customers a week! But how can this be possible?"

Training Expert: "There are several strategies that could be employed. They have to be specific to the challenge, which deliver immediate results and cater specifically to areas that have maximum impact. Typically, it begins by looking into the quality of the first appointment that your sales team gets. Are they qualified? Then it could branch out to the sales process as well as the hard and soft sales skills. I don't know just yet in which areas your team could benefit from sales training. However, with your permission, I would like to continue to ask...

As you can see, the process is natural and with feeling. The dialogue is non-threatening and comes across in the form of a conversation. Always remember, you are demonstrating empathy and emotion. Make sure to resist the urge to give away too much information and leave room for the customer to be curious about your solution.

As often as you can, sincerely let the customer know that you are pleased to help them, assure them that you are not put out by helping them, and don't negotiate your willingness to help with conditions attached. Do, however, remind them in a subtle way that you are in fact helping them. This is a classic example of anchoring the relationship.

Developing Your Questions

How many questions should you have for each meeting? A general rule of thumb is to have 1 question for every 2 minutes of sales time. As illustrated earlier in this chapter, for a one-hour meeting, you have approximately 45 minutes of selling time. Therefore, you should have 23 prepared questions as part of your toolkit. It's highly unlikely that you will get through all of your questions.

However, what's the downside of returning from war with spare ammunition in your gun? There isn't any.

At the beginning of this chapter, you wrote down as many questions that you could come up with. You wrote them down exactly as you ask them. Review that list and then separate your questions into "types". You probably have many "w" based questions. You may find that your questions reference the present versus past and future. Do you have enough questions to ask? In what order should you be asking these questions. Do you have Drill Down and Core Issue questions in your portfolio? Finally, do you have a protocol that you can follow that works for you?

Great questions to a sales expert are as important as tools are to a mechanic. You must have them to get the job done. Your high quality questions will separate you from your sales competitors and ensure more productive and successful sales meetings. By paying close attention to the different types of questions you ask, you will ensure that all the necessary information has been obtained to put together that effective final presentation.

Remember, the customer will only remember you by the quality of questions that you have asked.

Chapter Six

Your Own Extreme Sales Event

[Ed. Note- Larry Adams is the "go to" guy for an Extreme Event!]

An Extreme Sales Event is an event put on for your clients to create "Viral Marketing" - word of mouth excitement that travels from one prospect to another.

This is an event that creates memories and says "THANK YOU" to your clients. Setting up and running an Extreme Sales Event can separate you from the competition by making you the only Salesperson who does it. The Event creates a buzz about you and your business.

Expensive?

It doesn't have to cost you an arm and a leg to hold an event. It just has to come from inspiration that shows your clients you care enough about what you do to be different. An Extreme Sales Event helps you to be recognized as the best.

I'm not talking about a "SALE! SALE! SALE! EVERYTHING MUST GO!" sales event. I'm talking about using your imagination to produce an event that will create lasting memories for your clients; an event that will brand you as unique.

Four Steps to an Extreme Sales Event

> ➢ Inspiration
> ➢ Planning and Outsourcing
> ➢ Extreme Action
> ➢ Return and Report

Inspiration

Inspiration is something everyone is entitled to but few understand. We all have moments of inspiration where an idea pops into our heads. Those "Aha!" moments. The problem is that most don't act upon the promptings. We think, "Ah, what a cool idea." And then continue to go about our daily routines until the idea is lost from memory. One secret that separates the top producers from the rest of the pack is the ability to trust and act upon inspiration.

You must be open to inspiration in your work. You need to let your best ideas rise up and engage you in work that matters. Many just keep doing what they have always done and ignore those little ideas that could make their work remarkable. It's not that you aren't "an idea person" or that you don't receive inspiration; you just haven't learned how to recognize and act upon the promptings. I'm going to show you how.

The first thing you need to do is stop the loss of good ideas. We all have had great ideas come to us only to lose them because we didn't write them down. We think, "I'll write that one down when I get home," but we don't because when we finally do get home the grass needs to be cut, Tommy needs be taken to soccer practice and there are ten voice mails to run through. Before we know it, the idea has disappeared like all the other great ideas we never acted upon.

So what do you do?

Start an inspiration log.

Get a notebook that will be easy to keep with you. It could be a pocket size paper notebook or your PDA. What matters is that you have something with you to write down your ideas when they come to you. Remember, if you don't write it down…it's lost! This is why you should take notes whenever you go to a seminar. I have seen many participants go through a seminar and get totally pumped up only to go back to their same old routines two weeks later. Why? They never write down the important parts of the seminar that they could implement into their business. We often think that if it's really a great idea it will stick with us and that if we do forget about it then it must not have been such a great idea after all. That's just nonsense. Most great ideas start out as seemingly insignificant ideas that have been acted upon and then blossom into something remarkable.

I keep my main list of "Inspired Thoughts" on my laptop. Whenever I'm out and about and a thought comes to me I jot it down on my PDA (so that I don't lose it) and then I transfer it to my laptop during my planning time.

You should schedule time each day to plan and organize your work projects. I like to set aside at least a few minutes of quiet time each day for this purpose. This is the time to tap into your inspiration. Your inspiration log will be a great resource. Inspired thoughts are energizing. They engage your passion! Every day I look forward to reflection and planning. I love to run through my list of inspired ideas and decide how and when I will take action. Do you get to do what you love to do every day? Start working from inspiration and you soon will.

An important principle of engaging inspiration is to act upon the promptings we receive. When we act upon the prompting we have already received we are open to more promptings. When we don't record our thoughts, we forget them and our minds seem to be closed to future ideas. If, on the other hand, we write our ideas down and put them into action, we find that our minds are filled with more ideas. It's just like training a muscle - use it or lose it.

Here is an example of how this can work in the world of sales.

Banker who was inspired to put on an Extreme Sales Event

The banker was attending a program at her daughter's elementary school on child safety. The presenter mentioned it is important to have a Child Identity File for your child with current pictures and fingerprints. The banker agreed that it would be a good thing to have, but how do you get fingerprints? And then inspiration struck! What if she organized an after school workshop where parents could bring their children and make a Child Identity File?

She wrote her thoughts down and went to work. If she could organize the workshop for her daughter's school maybe she could do the same for other local schools. The idea was to put on a memorable event where parents and children could put together a Child Identity File. Then as they would leave, the banker would hand them a packet of all sorts of helpful information for parents, including a College Savings Account application from her bank.

The banker received a lot of help from the local PTA in putting together a wonderful packet of information that would be valuable to the parents. She called a police officer acquaintance and agreed to pay him $80 for a couple hours of his time. One of the teachers took all the pictures. It turned out to be an Extreme Event!

The banker was able to put on a memorable event that gave lasting value to the parents. The parents left with a Child Identity File and a packet of helpful resources. The children had fun doing an activity with their parents at their school. The local school came away looking good for hosting the event. AND, the banker walked away with over 50 good referrals! Now let's look at these referrals. The banker has made a great first impression. She has already given the parents something of value. The parents have a need to save for their child's education. That is just the beginning. Once a financial relationship is established with the parents through the College Savings Account, the banker may help the parents with other financial needs (retirement savings, loans, investments,).

That demonstrates how a little inspired thought can turn into an Extreme Sales Event - an event that is repeatable. Not only can the banker do it at other schools, but every year when new children flow into the school, it becomes an annual event. Perhaps the most important thing that happened is the banker learned how to act upon inspiration, which makes her open to future moments of inspiration!

Key Question: How would your life change if you were enabled to go from one inspired project to the next?

You would be doing what you do best. You would be the only one who does what you do and you would be producing some Extreme Sales!

Planning and Outsourcing

Once the original inspiration has given you the "Extreme Idea" for your event you should keep the channels open for more inspiration during your planning and outsourcing. These events take a lot of work and to pull them off as truly remarkable you must plan things out and get whatever help you can through outsourcing.

As you brainstorm your event keep good notes. A good exercise to do with your notes is to make columns for all the areas for which you need to keep track (questions and problems to solve, solutions, resources needed, outsourcing). Especially important is the "questions and problems to solve" column. As you plan your event, all sorts of questions and problems will pop into your head. If you make it a practice to write them down, two things will occur. First, you will open your mind to recognize any potential problems and second, you will ensure that you won't forget to come up with solutions to any situation that has already come to you.

As you plan, remember that this should be fun. You want your clients to connect with their emotions so that the event is memorable. I would go so far as to say that if you can't get excited about doing the event, STOP! Don't put your efforts into something that is not engaging your passion. Remember, you want to be exceptional. If you are passionate about your event the chances are that it will be extreme and you will be exceptional. No passion, no event! Period!

"OK", you say, "But Larry what if I'm in the middle of planning my event and it just isn't going anywhere? I can't get excited about my work and I'm starting to wish I hadn't started the project." Stop right there and do an assessment of your situation. Are you bogged down because the details are boring you or is the project just not worth doing? If it is just the hard work that concerns you, go back and remind yourself why you are putting on the Extreme Sales Event.

If the results have a good chance of being truly remarkable, then take courage from envisioning the end results and keep moving. If you are finding that the event just isn't going to be extreme, then get out before you waste more of your valuable time. Go back to your inspiration log and find another project. You need to know when to quit. If the project does not engage your passion, change it so that it does or STOP! Now, I'm not encouraging you to quit every time the road gets a little bumpy. I'm advising that you should not stick with something if it has shown you that it has little chance of being remarkable. Too many people hang on to a project because they have invested time into getting it up and going. If it isn't worth doing, then stop. There are a lot of great projects out there that are worth your time.

Help?

As you look for solutions and resources to resolve your questions and problems don't be afraid to ask for help. If you are excited about your project and your passion shines, there will be plenty of people willing to help. In the previous example the banker enlisted help from teachers, the PTA, the principal and a police officer. Most people love to help out when the feel that they are doing work that matters. If you have a passion for your project they will perceive helping you as work that matters. They will be glad to offer a helping hand.

Some things need to be outsourced. It is doubtful that the banker could have learned how to do finger prints in a satisfactory fashion. Outsourcing to the police officer was a good idea. It cost her some money but the referrals from the event will be worth the expenditure. If one of the items on your "problems that need to be solved" list can be done easier and cheaper by someone else, outsource it. Keep an eye out for those around you who have talents and abilities that can be put to use on your project.

One sales rep, John, who caters to law offices, found that he was being screened by the executive assistants to the partners of the law firms. It was very difficult to get in touch with the decision makers because the assistants handled all incoming calls. His efforts were concentrated on getting around the assistants with little success. Then inspiration came!

What if he established a trusting relationship with the assistants and made them his advocate?

Wouldn't this help him reach the decision makers? John knew he had little chance of establishing a relationship by standing in the reception area of the law firm so he came up with an idea to throw a luncheon for the executive assistants. He didn't want the luncheon to come off as a bribe so he decided to turn it into an extreme event.

John set up his planning notes and found solutions for the place, time and date of the event, but he just couldn't come up with an agenda to make it a WOW! luncheon. Because his mind was open to inspiration, he noticed a flyer for a local community college while visiting a client. The flyer had about five continuing education courses listed. A course on time management entitled "Don't Let the Clock Beat You!" appealed to John's senses. He contacted the professor who taught the course and inquired about hiring her to give a presentation at the luncheon. She was agreeable and available for the date needed.

John enlisted the help from one of the executive assistants in doing his PR work to build interest. He took the assistant to lunch and explained how he really wanted to make this exciting and valuable to the participants. His passion for wanting to create something special for her colleagues engaged her in the process. Not only did she talk the event up but she also put it on the agenda of the weekly staff meetings. She even helped John with some of the details of the luncheon.

The guest speaker was great and the event turned out to be quite memorable. John became exceptional in the eyes of those that attended. They appreciated someone putting on an event just for them. The information on time management was discussed during several staff meetings in the weeks following. Most important of all, John was always put right through to the decision makers whenever he called! He had become a trusted vendor in the eyes of the executive assistants and they were the gatekeepers.

John planned a great Extreme Sales Event and outsourced the agenda because he listened to inspiration and followed up with his passion. The event helped him make a lot of sales. Additionally, it was repeatable. He could do similar luncheons at other firms and make it an annual event by simply changing the workshop topic.

Extreme Sales Events can be a lot of fun and produce a lot of sales down the road. They can take a lot of work and you have to get your planning and outsourcing right. Don't hesitate to follow your inspiration. You may think that you can't pull something off like an extreme event, but if you follow your passion things will fall into place. You will be able to solicit help from others; and ideas for outsourcing will come your way. Don't be afraid to take action, or should I say, Extreme Action.

Extreme Action

Taking extreme action isn't impossible. Extreme action can be intimidating because it often takes you outside of your comfort zone. Everyone fears doing something no one else is doing because it can make him or her look bad if things don't turn out; but doing what no one else does is what makes you unique. Think of the alternative – doing what everyone else is doing.

You will never become exceptional doing what everyone else is doing. The exceptional dare to be different.

They know that if they can position themselves in the market as the only person who does what they do, they will take away the competition.

So how do you make sure you are taking extreme action? Every day during your planning and scheduling time, make sure to take some kind of action toward one of your inspired work projects. If your schedule doesn't include at least a third of your time devoted to inspired work projects then you probably aren't doing work that matters. Instead, you are doing what everyone else does. Most people busy themselves all day with things that really don't produce great sales. They work on answering emails, organizing the office, reading product information sheets, and cold calling; but they don't take the time to engage their passion. Don't do what most people do. Be exceptional!

If one third of your schedule is devoted to inspired work projects you are sure to become exceptional because you are doing work that matters - work that separates you from the competition; work that engages your passion and gives you the ability to stay energized while doing the other necessary activities of the day. Don't be afraid to take extreme action. It is the only way you will become the best at what you do.

When You Want the Whole Clinic...

There were fourteen doctors who worked for this practice and all of them worked with patients who had the potential of using the medicines she represented. Needless to say, this medical practice could become one of her best clients if she could become trusted as the rep of choice.

Sue had called upon the medical practice for about two years and had established a good working relationship. The problem was that she just didn't stand out ahead of the pack of other reps that called on the doctors. One day Sue was visiting the medical practice when she overheard a discussion about the annual picnic that had happened that weekend. The employees were complaining that the event had gone down hill the past couple years and they were considering canceling the plans for the future.

On her way home that evening while she listened to the radio in her car she thought, "Could I take on the planning of their annual picnic? What if I did and it turned out to be worse than this year's? That's just taking too big of a risk!" So, she put it out of her mind.

About a month later she was talking with a friend who had just attended the annual picnic for his employer. The picnic was a great success. He talked about all the different activities, the food, the great location and about the fact that they even had a band. The planning committee had gone out of their way to plan every detail and made it fun for the entire family. As he told her about all the activities that took place during the picnic, Sue began to wonder if she could pull off such an event for her client. She decided to take extreme action. She called the office manager and pitched the idea of letting her head up the annual picnic next year. The office manager was happy to let someone else take the burden and thought that it couldn't be any worse than it was this year. Sue was off and running.

Sue started her planning and made a list of questions and problems that would need to be resolved in order to pull off an extreme event. She scheduled some sort of action every week from the "solutions" column. Sue contacted her friend who told her about his awesome annual picnic and solicited his help. He agreed to meet with her over the next couple months to give suggestions and brainstorm ideas. He turned out to be a great resource.

Sue then started to hand out assignments to employees. Her passion soon caught on with the staff and she recruited plenty of volunteers to help pull off the extreme event. Her enthusiasm for the project was so well received that they gave her a larger budget than past events, which also allowed her to outsource the meal. She contracted with a local caterer (something that had never been done in the past) to furnish a great dinner. The activities were fun and many participated. Everyone went home with anticipation for next year's picnic. Sue had created an Extreme Sales Event!

Taking action on her inspired thought established Sue as exceptional. She was able to work with many of the employees during the planning and implementation of the event. The rest of the employees came to know her during the event. Now, when Sue visits the medical practice everyone calls her by name (something that doesn't happen to the other reps). Because Sue was willing to take extreme action, her sales increased and her manager noticed her efforts. She was assigned to two other large accounts. She is busy working on other inspired projects, which keeps her ahead of the competition. To her clients, she is the best in the world.

You can be the best in the world to your clients. Trust your inspiration and take some extreme action every day. Don't allow yourself to be satisfied with mediocrity. Be exceptional!

Return and Report

The last step is to return and report. This is where you consider all your notes, your plans and any feedback you have received and evaluate your Extreme Sales Event. Your goal is to build your confidence in taking on your next event. You have received inspiration and acted upon it. How did it go? Did your event help to make you exceptional? If not, what could you have done differently? What can you do today that will move you closer to completing your next event with even better results?

This time of reflection and evaluation is important in order to keep your passion engaged. You should take the time to celebrate the success and decide what actions you can take next time to avoid any bumps you might have encountered.

One way to get feedback is to hold a mini event to thank those who helped you with the main event. Take a group of those who helped you to lunch and have a celebration. They will appreciate the effort and will be more willing to help at your next extreme event. During the celebration ask questions. Find out how they feel about the event. Take notes so that you can use them during the planning for the next event. Don't forget to send a thank you card to everyone that attended your event.

Another way to ensure that you have a method to collect feedback is to always get the email addresses of the volunteers. You will need their email address to communicate during the planning and implementation of the event. During the return and report phase you can send out a short survey asking for their sincere input on all aspects of your event. The return emails can be extremely valuable in helping you to plan for your next event.

One last example

A sales rep named Ron was asked by a client to sponsor "a hole" in their annual golf outing for the last several years. The outing raised money for a local charity and had built up a big following. The rep didn't mind spending the money but felt he wasn't getting much bang for the buck. Instead of pulling out of the event and taking the chance of offending his client, Ron decided to turn his sponsoring of a hole into an Extreme Sales Event. He made some phone calls and found a local club pro who was a long hitter and great off the tee. The rep hired the pro for the day of the outing.

Ron called up the head of the planning committee and asked to sponsor the 306-yard par four. He then told the committee that he would bring in a golf pro who would take any participant's tee shot for an additional $10 donation. The committee agreed due to the potential of raising more money.

What happened was remarkable. The pro was in his groove that day and was putting three out of four balls on the green. This allowed many of the teams to putt for eagle. It was a great demonstration and everyone enjoyed watching a real pro tee up and hit their ball. All the teams were amazed at the pro's accuracy and the hole raised a lot of money for the charity.

Ron received the best Return and Report anyone could receive. They liked his Extreme Sales Event so much that he was asked to be on the planning committee for the next year's golf outing. This gave Ron many opportunities to be in front of new prospects. He made many great contacts and referrals. In the eyes of his client he became exceptional.

When can you run your first Extreme Sales Event? It's time to sit down and put some inspired projects on your schedule. Take action today so you can be exceptional tomorrow. There's no time to waste doing the same thing everyone else is doing. Make yourself unique. Become the only person who does what you do. Make Extreme Sales Events a part of your business and watch your prospects turn into profits!

Chapter Seven

Selling The Room – The Art of Mass Influence

[Ed. Note- Dave Lakhani is one of the finest salespeople on the planet at the front of the room. No one writes about selling to groups...except Dave...]

This may well be one of the most technical chapters of this book. I'm going to lead you through a process that I've used hundreds of times in hundreds of boardrooms worldwide to close millions of dollars of sales. I'm not going to motivate you or pump you up. I'm going to give you a step-by-step process to **create results with groups**, like never before.

We've all been there, a conference room filled with expectations and competing agendas and just one person responsible for bringing them together and orchestrating a profitable outcome.

You.

Selling the room is one of the toughest challenges in sales because even when you've correctly identified the decision maker you've still got to persuade the influencers and the silo builders. You have to overcome the old relationships and the new ones some of the group have already invested in emotionally.

It is a little like running the gauntlet in the old Cowboy and Indian movies.

And while it may be frightening at first, it is actually easier than a one on one sale if you understand the basics of mass influence.

Position and Package Your Self

Group judgments are quick and often harsh. You must set yourself up to be accepted immediately by the group rather than have them find you incongruent and pick you apart rather than focus on the solution.

Dress for your presentation. In an age of business casual a suit stands out and commands authority. It is a uniform and a clear indicator of who is in charge in the room. Use it to unconsciously control your environment from the very beginning.

Develop powerful stories that incorporate the use of testimonials of like businesses or like business problems that you've solved. Make sure each story has a build up to conflict and obvious resolution. Demonstrate how you've been personally involved in managing and seeing the successful implementation through.

Use *simple* PowerPoint slides that quickly and clearly communicate your point. Where possible, provide proof using audio and video to deepen the experience and to set you apart from other salespeople who will bring one-dimensional PowerPoint if at all. Remember that PowerPoint was developed for storyboarding, the very powerful technique used by filmmakers and other visual communicators to present messages in easy to understand segments. Present your most persuasive segments leading into your close.

Use very precise language. Don't stutter, stammer or use a lot of filler words. Focus on clarity of communication, creating big emotional word pictures and be to the point. People will make the simplest and most obvious choice provided to them. Lead them.

DIVIDE AND CONQUER

A basic tenet of mass persuasion is that what you do to one you do to everyone who is emotionally invested in the outcome of the problem at hand. If you gain the compliance of one it is much easier to gain the compliance of the rest of the group.

In every group there is a consensus creator, someone who is the leader in the room that everyone looks to. Own that person and you own the room. Don't be fooled, the highest ranking person in the room is probably NOT the person gathering consensus; their job is to simply take the recommendation of the group or be the person who asks hard questions. Identifying the consensus creator is relatively easy. It comes from asking questions and watching the responses.

In order to identify who the consensus creator is, lead by asking questions that require identification of a problem on the buyer's part. Here are a few powerful questions to ask to ferret out the consensus creator.

Who here has been responsible for gathering the ideas of the group and bringing everything together to date?

What conclusions have you come to as they relate to the solutions presented so far?

If you could wave a magic wand and have the perfect solution, what would it be? (Ask this question to everyone individually in the room.)

When you think about these possibilities, what is most important? (Here is where you will see the consensus creator leap into action).

Once you see who is taking the lead in creating consensus, you now know whom you need to influence. That person becomes your focus, get buy in from them and they'll get buy in from everyone else.

Communicate and Control

Reflective listening is a key in this stage of the game. Reflect back to the consensus creator what you heard them say was agreed upon; get their agreement, along with the group's agreement that you understood them.

Buy in comes when you present information to a person who is gathering consensus in the way that best represents the consensus that was created. So, when you present an idea or solution, you present it to the consensus creator and ask them if the idea or solution meets their understanding of what was earlier agreed upon.

A key point in deeply influencing the consensus creator is acknowledging their power. Ask them to confirm that the idea or solution is what meets the group's needs as identified by the group. Let them bring it to the group and confirm it.

When you are ready to present your most powerful points or ideas, do it not from the front of the room, but from the side of the consensus creator. Go and stand next to them, place your hand lightly on their shoulder if they are sitting or stand directly next to them shoulder to shoulder, lightly touching or nearly touching and make your point. Communicate from their vantage point and to the point of view of the rest of the room.

When you partner with the consensus maker, you assume their ability to bring about a conclusion and you get them emotionally involved with you.

Touch and Move to Deepen Rapport

In boxing, "to stick and move," is to throw a punch and move.

In selling the room we want to move through the room and make physical contact with people throughout the room.

One of the biggest mistakes that salespeople make is not being in physical contact with their audience. Humans crave human contact, it connects you if only temporarily and it interrupts the internal dialog so that their focus is shifted to you.

When I elicit information from people I nearly always touch them. One of the best places is on the shoulder and/or back of the arm if they are sitting or on the elbow if they are standing. I'll often touch the elbow or shoulder and hold the touch while I ask the question, I'll then remove the touch as they speak and then touch them again briefly when I thank them or encapsulate their answer.

The key to touch is not to overdo it. It shouldn't look or feel forced and it shouldn't be excessive. Just a few brief, natural connections that allow the person to know you are there, that you care about them and that you are focused on them.

Creating Buy In

Your audience needs to see you as someone like them, someone focused on understanding their needs and someone committed to helping them find a perfect or near perfect solution.

> *The audience needs to feel your empathy as they describe the pain and challenges that they've experienced that led them to this point and that they've experienced as they've explored all of their options.*

They need to accept you as their solution provider. And you create that acceptance by using a combination of three powerful persuasion tactics:

Leverage social proof

Social proof is demonstrating the effectiveness of your solution by showing other people who are doing exactly what you are suggesting. It is much easier for people to make a decision or create a change when they see someone else doing what they are considering effectively and profitably. Demonstrate that you and your solution are trustworthy by showing them your solution in action through testimonials, video, and if necessary or practical by taking them physically to the location where they can experience your solution in action, allow them to talk to a customer live. Demonstrate your solution so that they can see it in action.

Experience the solution

The deepest levels of persuasion occur when someone experiences something on their own. Their personal experience overrides experiences reported or explained by others and their own experience becomes reality. Experiential persuasion is personally defendable persuasion. The person experiencing the persuasion will defend their belief to the end. They are emotionally committed to the belief. The sooner you engage the audience by getting them involved in your presentation, the faster you'll sell. Engage the group in discussing how they could see your solution working in their organization. Get the consensus creator to help solidify the ideas. Use brainstorming and creative problem solving to get everyone to develop ways that your product will produce the results they need.

Set the criteria

Jointly set the criteria by which success will be determined. Setting criteria is powerfully persuasive as it is creating a commitment to how the project will be run and judged in terms of its successfulness. You are also leading the process of creating the criteria and you are able to carefully craft it to be unmatched by your competition. Make the criteria as specific as possible for best results, particularly in areas where your solution has a competitive advantage over another potential supplier.

Create the future now

Have them begin describing either verbally or in writing, in the present tense, what their organization will look like using your solution as it solves their problem. For example, a statement they might use would be "Distribution is now delivering all shipments twenty percent faster with an average daily savings of five hundred dollars on shipping." I often frame this as an exercise and I'll say "Here is what I'd like to have everyone do, grab a piece of paper and write down in the present tense what your organization would look like after implementing our solution." Then, have them read them out loud and get the consensus creator involved in narrowing them down to the single most powerful outcome that they've experienced by implementing your solution.

By getting "buy in" from the participants, you get them to accept you as their solution provider. In this effort you've now created a level of intensity in the room that none of your competitors have. You own the audience and at this point you'll have to really do something out of sorts to get them to change their mind about you.

Intensify Emotional Connectedness

Once you've gotten buy in, reinforce what you've created together. Start by reviewing the criteria you've developed. Second, deepen the connection by offering to do something in the spirit of collaboration "even though you know that they still need to see other vendors." Get them to commit to some follow through actions based on your shared understandings from the presentation. By getting them engaged in implementing some ideas with you, you get them to fully accept you as their solution. You go from demonstrating for them to leading them.

Create and Maintain Buying Pressure

One of the elements that I almost always see missing in selling the room is the structured call to action.

A structured call to action is one that is built around the elements of your presentation to the room that leads to a natural conclusion by the group. It may also include discounts, bonuses for early action or other incentives to buy.

"Buying pressure" is initiated by gaining agreement throughout your presentation.

The more the buyers agree, the more committed they become to the solution.

Here is what the maintained buying pressure sequence looks like:

> ➢ Gather agreement early that your solution can or will work for them.
> ➢ Intensify the pressure by getting them to describe in the present tense what the applied solution looks like.
> ➢ Hint that you'll be revealing something that will make this the most obvious choice they've ever made.
> ➢ Overcome objections and gather commitment.
> ➢ Reveal the first bonus, price drop, concession, etc. Let them know how important developing a relationship is (notice I didn't say how important their business is) and that you want to demonstrate your commitment to them.
> ➢ Offer them an opportunity to come to a buying decision.
> ➢ If there is resistance, offer any other fast action bonus items, other price considerations, special incentives, etc.
> ➢ Close again.
> ➢ If necessary, create a break and bring the most interested people around you so you can close them individually or as a group and get their commitment to driving the deal forward. Create value for them individually, help them advance their agenda and get their needs fulfilled.
> ➢ Close the group as a whole again with the help of your supporters.

In many corporate organizations, making a decision immediately may not be allowed. They may require that a certain number of vendors be consulted or that the group meet again before making a buying decision in order to compare all their options. If this is the case, you can intensify the buying pressure by taking away some incentives if the decision is not made in a certain period of time. This will often get them to get to the review stage more quickly.

You'll also want to stay in close contact with the key influencers in the room and the consensus creator to keep the emotional connectedness high.

Primacy and relevancy will play a key role in the decision process when they consider the alternatives. The solution with which they had the most recent exposure will be the one that is most often compared against unless it was clearly not a fit. Your job is to be sure that you speak with the buying group or your supporters just before their meeting to review the key points of your solution that they found most compelling.

Since you often won't get the chance to do this in person, I either do it by phone or by creating a simple video which I'll upload to my website or to Google Video and send that to them. The video will be short and to the point, no more than two or three minutes long and I will go over all of the most important points, make comparisons to other solutions I know they are reviewing and resell them on the value proposition of my solution. That person-to-person connection will often be enough to reengage the emotional connectedness and commitment to your product that will pull you through the review process and have you come out the obvious solution.

High quality video can now be created using a simple pocket camera like the Canon SD1000. It is a point and shoot camera that does video at 30 frames per second or faster. It records to digital media, which can be easily transferred to your computer and uploaded to your site or Google Video.

Big Effort Yields Bigger Rewards

Selling to the room requires a lot of preparation, a focused and planned presentation and often tremendous amounts of follow up.

By understanding the process and selling using a proven plan you'll tip the scales in your favor and you'll stand out in a crowded marketplace full of seemingly similar solutions.

But your professionalism, preparedness and relevant solution will carry the day.

PART TWO:
THE INNER GAME

Chapter Eight

Fueling Sales with Value-Driven Selling

[Ed. Note- Dr. Mollie Marti lives many lives. Salesperson, Social Psychologist, Consultant, Coach and Attorney (An attorney is ironically a.k.a. a "solicitor" in the United Kingdom).]

This book is written for people in sales. If you are reading this book, that means *you*! How do I know this? Because *everyone is in sales.* We are all in the business of communicating, persuading, negotiating, and influencing other people. Sales professionals sell specific products to their clients while clergy sell salvation to parishioners, authors sell ideas to their readers, teachers sell knowledge to students, recruiters sell their program to participants and mediators sell peaceful solutions to parties in dispute. Even parents sell their value systems and philosophies to their children. Throughout the course of each day, you inevitably spend substantial time and effort trying to sell to others something that is important to you. Working to manage other people's impression of you is a form of sales. You might not make a living in sales, but you will be selling something your entire life.

If you think you are an exception to this rule then it may be because you do not believe that you are good at selling. Don't equate not liking something or lacking certain skills with not doing the activity at all. How good do you think you are at sales? Are you an effective communicator, able to persuade and influence others and consistently find resolutions that mutually benefit you and others? If you need to improve in any area of sales (and who doesn't!), this book is full of tools, strategies and tips to increase your effectiveness. So block off the time, roll up your sleeves and get to work improving your sales skills.

Think about the different venues in which you are going to use your sales skills. The possibilities are endless. With some personal reflection and an understanding of establishing a value-based direction, you can identify the areas of sales in which you can make a unique contribution and be rewarded accordingly. When you use values as the foundation for your selling, you unleash the power of selling as your genuine, authentic self. This shift frees up energy formerly used to try to be who you thought others wanted you to be or say what you thought others wanted to hear. Selling from a solid foundation of knowing yourself, what you value and how you want to behave will make you more successful in sales. You also will experience a high degree of fulfillment and wake each day knowing that you are living a life perfectly designed for you. How powerful is that!

This chapter focuses on helping you identify your values and commit to using them as the basis for all decisions in your life, including how you want to use your sales skills. Will using the process set forth below provide clarity about what you truly want to do – and not do – with your life? Yes. Will it make it easier to focus on your priorities and improve your performance? Yes. Will it enable you to see the old excuses and bad habits that get in the way? Yes. You probably will discover that you are doing some things that do not serve your life purpose. This process will make it easier to say yes to things you want in your life – and no to other people's priorities. You can use it to identify your purpose, integrate all facets of your life, wake every morning motivated to become a better version of yourself, produce amazing results and find great fulfillment within each day. Let's get started.

Value-Driven Vs. Goal-Driven

In order to maximize motivation, your daily sales priorities need to be based on one thing: your values. Values are subjective beliefs about what is important to you and that you see as acceptable to others. In order for you to perform at a high level continuously, you need to use your values as the foundation of your professional – and personal - life.

How are you doing so far with all of this talk about "values"? Are you nodding your head in agreement – or quickly tuning out? The word does have a warm, fuzzy feel to it. Goals are so much more concrete. We are taught from early on that setting and reaching goals drives results. Some people actually come to believe that their goals *are* their values. They get addicted to setting and achieving goal after goal, never stopping to establish a solid foundation for their tenacious goal setting. It is not that these people do not have values. They simply have not taken the time to think through what is truly important to them and to link what they do on a daily basis to these foundational principles.

From a motivational perspective, it is essential to distinguish between living a value-driven life and a goal-driven life. The danger of a goal-driven life is that once you achieve a goal your body will stop producing energy. Your body abides by the *law of conservation*. This means that you will only expend as much energy as you believe is necessary to achieve the task at hand. When your goal is achieved, your body will say that it has given enough energy and will go flat. In order to get back up, it is necessary to hurry and set the next big goal. Given the emphasis on setting and achieving goals in the sales industry, sales professionals are at a particular risk for falling into a goal-hopping pattern.

Over time, a pattern of hopping from goal to goal without a connection to underlying values can lead to a great sense of emptiness and loss. The news frequently reports on how someone who has been extremely "successful," judged by achieving one goal after another, gives up on their profession or even life itself. Examples can be found in every area, from successful business people and politicians to famous athletes and celebrities. This makes no sense to those on the outside looking in, who are thinking that person has it made. What more could they want? The goal-hopper also is confused, and the question he is asking himself is, "Look at all I have achieved. How can I feel so empty inside?" Often times this searching is accompanied by various types of addictions, serving as a coping mechanism to try to fill the emptiness. Although these issues admittedly are multi-dimensional, an important aspect is the lack of a meaningful and value-based foundation for one's efforts. All of the money in the world will not motivate a person who has accomplished goals and has no values to fall back on. When a goal is completed, energy drops and production comes to a screeching halt.

The unique and immense power of values comes from their ongoing nature. They provide support and continuity because they are never completely fulfilled. Suppose that you value contribution. You need to give back in order to be truly fulfilled. Will you ever get to a point where you feel you have done enough? No, this value is ongoing so your body will continue to produce energy. You will not wake up one day and think, "Wow. I am really a giving person. I have made such amazing contributions to the world. Goal reached. Great job. I'm done!"

Another powerful aspect of using values as the basis for your motivation is that as you grow in your values, you get rewarded along the way. So if you value contribution and you give to another, you feel great and want to take your giving to the next level. As you embody more and more of this value by becoming an even more giving person, your experience of giving becomes deeper and richer. This type of deep fulfillment provides additional motivation to continue your growth.

The quickest measure of whether you are living a value-based life is to ask these questions: Do the things you do on a daily basis fulfill you? Do you love sales as much or more than as when you first started in your career? Is it fun for you? Do you enjoy sharing a product you believe in and taking on the challenges of persuading others to see the value of the product and how it meets their needs and desires? Do you roll with the ups and downs, understanding that you won't persuade everyone for a variety of reasons so you don't take rejection personally? Do you love the process and are energized by knowing that when you make a sale you have improved life for both your client and yourself? If selling in your venue is no longer fun (or never was) then it is time to make a change. Life is simply too short to spend a vast number of your hours doing something you do not enjoy. So let's take a closer look at the process of selling based on your values.

Establishing a Value-Based Direction

A useful metaphor for establishing your direction is planting a tree and watching it grow. Establishing your direction is a four-step process that begins with planting your values, grows upward through the trunk of your vision, extends through the limbs of your goals, and comes to fruition with your daily activities.

Step 1: Plant your values.

What attributes are integral to the life you want to live? You want to identify these as your *core values*. A "core" is at the center of something. Core values are those beliefs that originate at the core of your being. They are at the center of who you are as a person. Core values must be so essential to your life that you would not be *you* without embodying them.

To get you started in identifying your core values, following is a list of values from clients who have gone through this process. Take a minute to review this list. Which values speak to you?

Discipline	Adventure
Love	Competitiveness
Creativity	Financial Security
Tolerance	Happiness
Responsibility	Family Security
Friendship	Faith
Contribution	Inner peace
Honesty	Integrity
Loyalty	Humor
Learning	Compassion
Excellence	Spirituality
Self respect	Humility
Wisdom	Work Ethic
Health	Joy

Now take a closer look at the list. It is not enough to ask whether or not you think these attributes are good things. Each of the above values has positive aspects. You want to identify those values that are critical to your being and influence everything you do in all areas of your life, professionally and personally. They define you as a spiritual being and are the "soul" of who you are as a person.

There are many exercises to help you identify your values. When doing these exercises, you might want to create a quiet environment that puts you in a frame of mind for this deeper type of self-reflection. One exercise is to write

104

out your own obituary, as you would want it to appear in the newspaper after you have lived the life of your dreams. Write it in the third person, as though someone else is writing about you. You might want to take an additional step and boil down the summary of your life to a few brief words you would like to be written on your tombstone. When you have finished these exercises, take a break and then later review what you have written with fresh eyes. What jumps out at you as those things you really want to be or do in life that, if you died tomorrow, would be left undone?

On a lighter note, envision in vivid detail a birthday celebration 25 years in the future. Imagine that you are surrounded by the most important people in your life. These people are going to give a toast to you, briefly telling you what you have meant to them. Who is at this party? You might not know the exact person, but you can define the important roles you want to fill in your life, both personally and professionally. Is there someone attending who reflects your role as a salesperson, manager, co-worker, spouse, parent, sibling, client, friend, volunteer, or other role? Next, detail what you would like each speaker to say about you. How have you made a difference in their lives?

In my experience, people generally identify 15-20 core values. You might have more or less. Once you have your list, provide a short definition of what each value means to you. If you value humor, does that mean that you want to be a good joke-teller, that you want to laugh a lot or that you want to find humor within daily situations? If you value adventure, does that mean that you want to take big risks, want to travel the world or want to learn something new every day? There are no right or wrong answers. This is your life and these are your values. Define them to be true to yourself.

You might be sitting there thinking that this all sounds good but you already know what you are about and certainly do not have the time to sit down and work through any of these exercises. I have been there. And I can clearly remember when I did take the time to create my value list and direction piece. I already had accomplished much in my life and thought I knew what was important to me. But I had never taken the time to think through *exactly* what I was about. What explicit words did I want to use to fully define the person I knew I was being called to be? I walked around in a haze of deep thought and excitement for days as I did some of this "heavy" work. In helping others through this process since then, I have received many calls from some very successful and "busy" people who exclaimed as soon as I answered my telephone, "I just discovered another of my core values!" This is a cool and worthwhile process. Are you really so busy that you can't take time for *your life* and work through your values on paper?

Once you have defined your core values, play around with organizing them in a way that makes sense to you. Many people find it useful to organize them into families or some sort of prioritization scheme. You might have a family or group of values related to your professional life, personal relationships, community and spirituality. Only you have the answers to what structure best suits your value list.

Step 2: Envision Your Values in Action

You now have given thought to what values will serve as the foundation for your life. In setting forth your core values, you have identified the essential, ongoing principles upon which you want to base your life. Living your values on a daily basis will help motivate you and fuel the achievement of your "life visions.

Core values run so deep that when you use them to anchor your life, they serve as a steady source of guidance, no matter what life brings. Yet, values are intangible and some days it seems there are miles between the loftiness of these universal principles and the realities of your life. How do you consistently live your values on a daily basis? The answer lies in developing a *vision of your values in action.*

Your visions (or dreams, if you prefer) represent a picture you create in your mind about your future. These pictures energize you and provide a target to work toward. When you create a vision, you become clear about the character traits you want to possess, the achievements you want to attain, and the contributions you want to make. This process will help you crystallize the desired results for your life in the years to come.

You will have different visions for different aspects of your life, such as career, family and community involvement. If you have organized your values into families, then begin by creating your vision of each of these groups of values in action. Do you want to be the best sales profession that you can be, own your own company, run a marathon, have a more intimate relationship, or become financially secure? Notice how each vision can serve as an outlet for several values simultaneously. For each vision, indicate which values it fulfills. How will working toward that vision make you more of the person you want to become?

Re-read that last sentence and the power it contains. When your vision is value-based, as you work toward living your vision, you become more of what you value. In other words, you will become more financially secure, compassionate, honest, hard working, wise, have more integrity - whatever it is you value.

Creating and striving toward your visions moves you forward toward living your values and embodying more of each core value. The next step in making your values more concrete is goal setting. Up to now, we have talked only about a level of achievement. Goals provide more specificity by focusing on the achievements themselves. For example, your vision statement might state, "I envision being a sales professional with a large following of loyal clients who rave about my advice and service." A supporting goal statement might be, "By

June of this year, I will have increased my client base by ten percent with an average amount of X dollars in sales." Let's now discuss some parameters for effective value-based goal setting.

Step 3: Set Goals

In each of your visions, there will be a subject. You might envision being a top sales professional, having a close-knit family, owning your own company, being a published author, or competing in triathlons. You can use the subject matter (professional, family, authorship, health) to start a family of goals. These goals should support and direct you toward your vision, just as your vision supports and directs you toward your values.

It is beyond the scope of this chapter to detail guidelines for crafting effective goals. There are many books and online sources that will walk you through basic concepts such as being specific, making goals measurable, staying positive and setting timeframes. While you want to make sure you are effectively framing your goals, the focus of this chapter is showing the importance of using your value-based vision to set your goals.

Start by setting long-term goals that represent a means to fulfill your value-based vision. I define long-term goals as those set approximately one year away. It is rare to be able to set a high quality goal that sits out much farther than one year. With the technological advances, changes in personal circumstances, and general speed of life in the 21st century, setting a specific five-year goal could end up actually limiting your performance. For example, I knew as a college freshman that I wanted to become a lawyer. Had I set a seven-year goal to become a lawyer and mapped out the specific process, I would have missed out on the opportunity that presented itself in college to graduate in three years and spend the following year in Ireland. In law school, I would have missed out on a tremendous opportunity to clerk for a United States Court of Appeals judge who became one of my life's greatest mentors. When starting law school, much less when starting college, I did not even know a law clerk position existed or what needed to be achieved during law school to obtain a clerkship. Do not set an overly specific long-term plan for your life. This will limit you. Rather, set a series of goals no longer than one year in length, which can be renewed in order to achieve your vision.

I think of long-term goals as stretch goals, having at least a 50% probability of attaining them. Your visions are big so the initial goals you set to achieve them also need to be big. Long-term goals are the place to extend yourself. At this point you know "what" you want to achieve, but not all of the "how" you are going to do it. Do not let this stop you. Start making a concrete plan to reach toward those visions and you will set shorter-term goals to fill in the gaps along the way.

When setting long-term goals, you might want to use the phrase, "in my best efforts." When looking so far down the road, it is more likely that things can happen that are out of your control. Do not punish yourself if this happens. Say you set a long-term goal that states, "In my best efforts, by the first day of September, I will have qualified for Million Dollar Roundtable." In the meantime, your office is wiped out by a natural disaster and it takes six months to recover as many records as possible and get your office set back up. As dramatic as it sounds, I know a sales professional who was put in this position in New Orleans after Hurricane Katrina. He could not get back in his office for months. His paper files were destroyed. Most of his money was tied up in non-liquid assets like his house, which sat on the market for months as the housing market crashed. Life happens.

This example highlights the resilience that a value-based direction can provide. Setbacks of this caliber naturally are accompanied by a great deal of disappointment. These experiences could be absolutely crushing to someone who had valued the goal itself. They would be focused on the unachieved goal and not the fact that they gave their best and full efforts to living out their values. The sales professional in New Orleans, on the other hand, had established a strong value-based life direction. While licking his wounds, he was able to fall back on his underlying vision of being the best sales professional that he could be. This vision softened the blows. It provided a cushion upon which he could land, more quickly establish new goals as alternative outlets for his values and begin all over again.

After you establish your long-term goal, set shorter term goals such as six-month or quarterly goals. These goals may be renewed several times in order to achieve a long-term goal. I think of short-term goals as having at least a 75 percent probability of attainment. You still need to work to achieve them, yet they are more realistic than long-term goals because of the shorter time frame.

Short-term goals need to be sufficiently challenging without creating too wide of a gap between where you are and where you want to go in the near future. Say that you currently make $100,000 in annual sales and are not going to make any major changes in the near future (e.g., additional education, acquiring a mentor, restructuring daily activities). You might find setting a quarterly sales goal of $30,000 to be challenging and motivating, while setting a quarterly sales goal of $60,000 feels too far out of reach. Usually you will achieve your visions more quickly when you set smaller goals and consistently build on your success. In the end, you will outperform those who dream so big that they continually fall short and eventually throw up their hands in surrender. Feel the excitement as you stretch, improve and grow in order to become a better version of yourself. Next we'll talk about how to make this process even more real by boiling down your short-term goals to daily priorities and tasks.

Step 4: Set Daily Goals

Daily goals are where the work gets done. Ask yourself what you need to do *today* to achieve your short-term goals. It is important not to create a massive and ongoing "to do" list that simply rolls things over to the next day when they are not accomplished. When you do this, you look at those same items that still have not been completed day after day after day. These types of lists can put you in overload and quickly decrease your motivation to achieve anything.

One key to achieving daily goals is to put the activity on the day that it needs to be accomplished. For example, it is Monday morning and a client calls to make arrangements for you to give an important business presentation to her company on Friday. With a traditional "to do" list, you would write, "prepare presentation" on your daily goals list. But because the speech is at the end of the week, you likely would not give any energy to beginning preparation. So this activity would roll onto Tuesday's list, and then on to Wednesday's list. The effect of looking at that "to do" activity, day after day, knowing that you have not done anything to accomplish it, would decrease your motivation.

By contrast, your daily schedule might include the following steps:

Monday: Select presentation topic and conduct research
Tuesday: Complete research and draft presentation
Wednesday: Edit and finish writing presentation
Thursday: Practice full presentation and prepare handouts
Friday: Make GREAT presentation!

You will set many of your daily goals at the time you set your short-term goals. Say you have a goal to make a certain level of sales in three months. Start by thinking through all the steps that are needed to accomplish the goal. Then you can work backwards from your goal deadline and schedule in all of the steps that you will need to take (e.g., prospecting calls, appointments, sales proposals, follow-up calls, closings) in order to make the sales and achieve your goal.

You will want to review your daily goals at the beginning of each week and add any additional ones at this time. Setting goals on a monthly basis is not frequent enough because too much changes within one month's time. Although a daily review is imperative, setting daily goals without a broader viewpoint limits your perspective. If you are living day-to-day, setting goals along the way, you likely are spending most of your time responding to other people's priorities rather than living your own. Because the issue of getting things done on a daily basis is so essential to sales success, a later chapter gives additional guidance on how to set and achieve daily priorities.

The benefits of achieving daily goals are numerous. First, it is personally rewarding. Every time you check off a completed activity, you release neurotransmitters in the reward center of your brain that relay the message, "This feels good!" This process helps increase your motivation by physiologically changing you so that you feel better. Second, accomplishing your daily goals ensures that you will accomplish your short-term goals . . . which gets you closer to achieving your long-term goals . . . which puts you on the path to achieve your value-based visions.

Lastly, but certainly not least, achieving your daily goals helps you become more of the person you want to become on a daily basis. This is the power of establishing a value-based life direction. By linking your vision and goals to your values, and taking daily steps forward to achieve these goals, you are moving toward your ideal self. You will be living your life in such a way that every day you more fully embody your core values.

Motivational Check Up

Just as it is important to regularly see your health professional for physical check ups, it also is essential to conduct motivational check ups. One of the most common motivational scenarios I hear from sales professionals is, "I use to enjoy my sales career but that is no longer the case. My production is down. It is no longer fun. How can I produce better results and get back to enjoying what I do?"

This chapter provides the first step in providing the answer to this type of question: establish your life direction. Have you been hopping from goal to goal without really taking the time to identify the values you want to serve as the foundation of your life? Do you need to give more thought to defining visions for who you want to become and what you want to achieve in all areas of your life? Or do you truly know what you want, but your goals do not support this larger vision? Are you spinning your wheels on a daily basis, feeling that you are not moving ahead toward realizing the life you want and deserve? Establishing and continually revisiting a values-based life direction can provide answers to all of these types of questions. Of course, if you have never enjoyed sales or your career, than the need to establish your life direction is even more pressing. Use this chapter as a map to help you clarify your core values and the ways in which you can be rewarded for making your own unique contribution to this world. Remember, we are all in sales. How are you going to make this work best for your life?

Another important place to look when you find yourself less effective or no longer enjoying the process is your strategy development and execution. If what you do no longer works, perhaps you have strayed from the basics or established patterns of what you know produces results? Or perhaps your field has changed around you and you have failed to keep up with the demands of these changes?

Even when you know what you want and what you need to do to get it, life happens. The demands of your day are immense. Is life continually throwing distractions and barriers in your way that are making you less effective and sapping the enjoyment out of what you do? This book introduces routines and how to use them to protect your strategies and keep you on task. Establishing routines can quickly make you more effective and put you in a position to perform at a higher level on a consistent basis.

Finally, if you have a well-established life direction and solid strategies and routines and still lack results and enjoyment, you need to take a close look at how you manage your time and energy. Even if you have the desire and direction to accomplish something, you may be going nowhere if you are depleting your energy without refueling. Do you constantly feel like you have "no time" to do the things you need or want to do in life? Do you feel tapped out, fearing that even a minor unplanned emergency might push you over the edge? No one can run on empty. You need to refuel your mind, body, emotions and spirit on a regular basis. You also need to prioritize your daily activities and exercise integrity to accomplish these tasks. This book also addresses the importance of managing your energy and your time.

Summary

Establishing a value-based life direction lays the foundation not only for a successful career in sales, but also a life of daily fulfillment. The process of building your life direction from ground up can seem daunting. It means that you have to decide where you want to go and you have to commit to getting there. This involves hard work. And yet, the payoffs are immense. These written words can not give true meaning to the level of success and fulfillment you will experience when you identify your purpose, integrate all facets of your life, and wake every morning motivated to become a better version of yourself. Begin mapping out your life direction today.

Chapter Nine

Identifying with Your Customer

[Ed. Note- No one is better qualified than Eliot Hoppe in communicating the power of identification. K.H.]

As you probably realize by now, selling can be fun, exciting and rewarding. In general, we are compensated for influencing and persuading others to use our products, services or solutions.

In most cases, we are hired by someone or a company to reach out to new prospects and book the appointment. When at the sales meeting with our customer, we begin to build rapport and trust, ask questions, uncover need and pain points, talk about our features, advantages and the benefits and then hopefully turn them into a customer. This is an example of a very simple sales process.

Of course, in addition to growing the account base, we are also asked to insulate our existing customer base from the competition. This is usually accomplished by high touch activity with the customer once the sale has been made and the customer is a user of our service or product. This mandate is pushed downward from the executive levels and it is clearly laid out that this is what sales people are expected to think, act and do. After all, the company is paying us to execute, arguably, the most important job in any organization.

The issue here is that we are constantly being asked to sell, sell, and sell. Our minds are programmed and conditioned to sell, sell, and sell. Many companies will have monthly, quarterly or annual sales incentives. To qualify or win, our results are measured on how much we sell. Even our sales managers meet with us weekly or bi-weekly in either one-on-one or general sales meetings to budget forecasts, revise forecasts and get up to date information on what we have sold. To cap it off, they probe further as to our activity and what we are prepared to commit to sell both in the short and long term.

As you can see, there is a very distinct pattern that begins to develop. It is what separates mediocrity from professionalism. The issue lies right between the ears and is an easy fix. The question is, what attitude are you taking with you into every sales call?

If you currently walk into a sales meeting with the notion of "selling something" or "closing the customer", stop it now. If you are in the habit of counting the commissions or celebrating the scope of the opportunity before, during or after the call, stop it now.

Your approach and presentation should be focused on "helping the customer" and your ultimate goal in the relationship is to become a "trusted advisor" and "confidant" within the account. Your goal is to build a relationship with the customer that becomes so powerful that you literally become a consultant, subject matter expert and "go to" person when any issues or questions arise. You really know this has been achieved when your customer is calling you for advice on unrelated business or personal issues. This chapter will tell you exactly how to accomplish this.

Mindset

Quite often, there is a mental block that sales reps get. It's the same mindset as you had of your grade school teachers. You never looked at teachers as people who had family and personal lives, yet thought that they lived at the school because they were there to teach you and that was it. You never saw them outside, in the mall, at church, in social circles or in the neighborhood. It was almost as if they were deflated at night and stored away only to be blown back up again to begin a new day ready to teach you again.

A similar mental block is what sales people can fall into with their customers. We see our customers at their office during business hours and become immune to the fact that they have personal and business lives as well. We become so fixated on ourselves and the sales quota that we forget that the person across the table has other (and sometimes better) things to do than meet with us.

What sales reps often overlook are the internal and external influences and challenges that the customer is facing. Once we begin to view ourselves from the client's perspective, a whole new picture of our customer begins to develop.

Imagine this. You have secured a sales appointment with a customer whom you have not met before. This has been achieved through a referral, cold call, association – it really doesn't matter how. The bottom line is that you and the client have never met before. You walk in and introduce yourself to the receptionist and ask for Mr. Jones. Now, while Mr. Jones is paged and on his way down to greet you, you are asked to wait "over there" in the common waiting area with the comfortable chairs, coffee table and magazines. At this point, you have some self-chatter and inner dialogue going on in your head. You may be thinking about the last call you came from, you may be thinking about what needs to be done once this call is finished or you may simply pick up one of those magazines and flip through a few pages.

Your customer however just received a phone call one hour earlier that there could be a potential mistake in judgment, which he was responsible for, that could potentially cost his annual operating budget $25,000.00. Now the customer receives the call announcing that you are waiting for him at reception. What is the most important thing on the customer's mind at that moment?

The example is to illustrate that there are other influences in the customer's business life. The sales call that you are going to have in a couple of minutes could be very low on the priority scale at that time. If we walk into this call with the mindset that we are going to sell something, what would be the odds of having a great meeting? If we went into the same appointment with the mindset that we were there to help the customer, you will get your customer to open up and even get the customer to expose the issue(s) at hand. Remember, we are not talking about sales techniques to get the customer talking; we are only focusing on your frame of mind at that moment.

Don't wait until you are in the waiting area to "be in the zone", but rather get your head into the game well in advance of parking your car. Nothing else should matter to you than helping the customer. At this point you will not even know how you can help them. That's fine. The fact remains that if your mindset is of that to help, than that will be conveyed without words, by your actions. This is the first step that cannot be compromised.

Customer Influences

Your customer is just like you. They have personal and business lives. At any time throughout the day, they can receive good news, bad news, be asked to make a decision, change strategies, execute on a directive, prepare, present, facilitate and the list goes on.

Here are four key business responsibilities and influences in your customer's business that you should take into consideration. It is important to realize that in many situations, these other variables can play a role in the overall decision to use your product, service or offering. These are daily functions and top of their mind priorities that your customer must deal with. You should consider these responsibilities while strategizing your pre call plan and pay close attention to your customer's responses during the sales call.

Internal Competition – this includes all the other internal departments within an organization who compete for budget dollars, recognition, control, projects, prime sponsorship, budget headcount and so on. Quite often, disputes between inter-departments can develop. Sometimes these internal influencers can impede or assist the decisions and outcomes directly relating to you generating the sale. The larger the organization, the more internal competition and politics you will encounter. Effective questioning and listening skills are extremely important to uncover signs of internal competition. At times, the customer will leak information in a subtle way and you need to pay attention to these nuances and read between the lines as to the answers that you are given. As you become closer to the trusted advisor status with your customer, internal issues within the account become a natural part of the relationship.

External Competition – this includes everyone else competing with your customer's company for market share. It includes anyone who is actively trying to grow his or her own customer base at the direct expense of your customer. Your customer at many different levels is trying to protect and insulate the competitors from poaching from their existing client base. Customer retention is a mission critical mandate to businesses of all sizes from small and medium sized businesses to large corporate clients. Every single client that is acquired is done so at a cost. This is called Cost of Acquisition. In many cases, customers are acquired at a loss and the break-even point of that customer becoming profitable could be several months or years. In most cases, the cost of retention is less than the cost of acquisition making competitive awareness very high on the corporate radar.

Results and Performance Metrics - this includes all deliverables that your customer is responsible for, measured on and quite often compensated for. Many managers and leaders in an organization receive some form of variable compensation, bonus or over ride for achieving and exceeding performance targets. This does not come easy for managers who are missing targets and estimates. Your customer must present, and be accountable for, results and performance metrics with immediate supervisors, bosses and executives. These meetings are typically scheduled and in many cases, hours of preparation must take place.

Personal Goals and Achievement – this is a very important, and often overlooked influence, which plays a significant part of your customer's decision-making process. Your customer seeks the same liberties and lifestyle benefits that you look for. They too are looking to be promoted and recognized by the executive, peers, family, friends and others from outside work.

It quickly becomes very clear as to where your first appointment with the customer could potentially rank on their priority scale. One thing for sure is that this call is extremely high on your list of priorities. Empathy can go a long way. At any time, including as you sit in the waiting area, something can blow up and overshadow your appointment, which to you is most important. Although you may not be highly ranked on the customer's appointment list that day, you can build up your value strategically whereby the customer begins to include you in their radar of importance and priority.

Buying vs. Selling

Here's a question. As a consumer, do you like to be 'sold' something or would you rather buy something?" If you answered, "I like to be sold something", my sincere unsolicited advice is to get out of sales completely. You will not be able to alter that strong conviction and will consistently default back to selling mode with customers.

If you answered, "I like to buy something", then you have the proper mindset. All you have to realize is that the vast majority of people like to buy versus being sold. Of all the times that I have asked this question during training sessions that I have conducted, I have only had two people ever tell me that they sincerely like to be sold. Both are no longer selling as a career and I would lump them into the less than one percentile of people who like to be sold. Therefore, it is paramount that you create the perfect buying environment for your customer. Why? Because your customer is no different than you.

People will buy from you if they like you.

Have you purchased something from someone that you didn't like? Odds are that at some point in time, you have. Typically, your viewpoint of that entire experience will have a story, which concludes without a solid foundation for any further activity.

In some cases, consumers can tend to tolerate chases in a retail environment and buy a product from someone that they may not like. In Enterprise and B2B sales, you are dead in the water if the customer doesn't like you. Why? Because there are too many choices for your customer to consider. There are other factors to take into account as well; however as a rule of thumb, if they don't like you, they will not buy from you.

You may have an example of when you had purchased something from someone that you didn't like. I purchased something from someone that I didn't like – a car.

I recall going into a new car dealership to buy a car for my wife. The sales person who was very knowledgeable about the product only spoke to me and ignored my wife. Repeatedly, I mentioned that this purchase was for her and that he should be directing all of his questions and suggestions towards her. To my amazement, he continued to speak at me making me uncomfortable and my wife quite upset because she felt slighted.

In the end, I still purchased the vehicle. As a consumer the deal was too good to pass up. It was nearly $11,000.00 off the list price. It was the last one on the lot. There were other people looking at it and surely they were going to buy.

It was a classic example of when consumers will in fact tolerate unprofessional behavior and purchase something from someone (the sales person, clerk, or merchant) who they don't really like. Here are the factors that will influence you to buy off someone that you don't like.

- ➢ Location – proximity to you, convenience
- ➢ Availability – The last one, one of few
- ➢ Offer – Limited time, price, bonus
- ➢ Post Sales Service – if required or not required

It is easier to be sold by someone that you don't like when two or more of the above factors become part of the decision to buy. In my case, I was motivated by the offer and law of scarcity – only one left. Although the new vehicle required scheduled maintenance, I had two dealerships closer to where I lived that could handle the service.

First Impressions

Your customer has now opened the door and you have made eye contact with him. You have not uttered a word and have not shaken hands. The most that you may have done at this point is smile and four seconds have passed. In those four seconds, your customer will have come to a few conclusions about you including; do I like this person and do I trust this person. Studies have also proven that the outcome of a long-term relationship can be accurately determined during those first four seconds. In other words, the outcome of the meeting and long-term relationship is strongly influenced in those first few seconds. What we do next will continue to add or subtract points on the customer's virtual "likeability scorecard".

It is at this point and time that we now say hello and shake hands. By this time a few more conclusions about you will be drawn. When you shake your customer's hand and you have a dry and firm handshake, you will be immediately scored well on the virtual scorecard, as you are perceived to be professional and confident. Should you have a clammy and limp handshake you will lose points on the virtual scorecard and be perceived as nervous and insecure. The intonation of your voice and how you introduce yourself will also add or subtract points on your virtual "likeability scorecard". The volume, pace and clarity of your speech is also being judged. I can recall several times where sales reps would introduce themselves to me and I would have to ask them to repeat themselves because the volume was low and they spoke too quickly. Asking a sales rep to repeat himself once is fine, however if the customer is asking questions repeatedly you are losing points very quickly.

There is also another influencer that is part of the bigger picture that you must not forget. It is the receptionist who asked you to sit down and wait when you first arrived. You should realize that those eyes have also been judging you and the opinion of that person could matter significantly down the road. Quite often, your customer will solicit feedback from others about you. Both receptionists and assistants must not be overlooked in the overall picture, especially in the beginning of any relationship.

The Likeability Scorecard

As account managers when selling our services to others, many times we classify our accounts into A, B and C candidates based on the volume of business the account generates. This then can influence the frequency of contact that we must maintain within the account throughout the year. Other factors which influence the ranking of an account would be if the customer were a champion, spokesperson, reference or contributor to future business. If you are familiar with Paretto's 80/20 rule, than it states that 80% of your business will come from 20% of your customers. If this was the case in your situation, you may have your A candidates represent the top 5% of your 20% base. Your B candidates probably make up the remaining 15% of the top 20%. Your C candidates probably make up the remaining 80% of your base.

Your customer is no different when meeting with you. You are being judged and ranked on a "Likeability Scorecard". Their ranking system on the scorecard is a series of plus and minus counts that draw some form of conclusion about you and the viability in extending the relationship. I recall asking one of my closest customers what he thought of me and my service. He mentioned that I was ranked a Sales Expert in his scorecard. I was flattered and asked if that was the highest level on his scorecard. He said yes. The other two rankings were Sales Pro and Sales Rep. He went on to say that Sales Reps did not get a second meeting. Sales Pro's did get the second meeting and sometimes the sale. The Sales Expert got the sale and the trusted advisor status.

To be viewed in such high regard in your customer's eye is golden. So what can we do to ensure that we consistently score high? The answer is a lot. There are many factors that must be demonstrated, sustained and reinforced throughout the relationship, the initial meeting and subsequent meetings - if you get one.

Trust

Demonstrating trust has to be the highest ranked element that you can convey to your customer. The simplest way to convey trust is to simply do what you said you were going to do. Trust is earned and not assumed. What we say and do affects our overall likeability scorecard. Your customer is constantly evaluating you and your trustworthiness during your sales call. Once the meeting has concluded, everything that you promised to do and achieve is scrutinized. Committing and delivering to agreed timelines, performance results and service agreements builds trust.

Be careful to not make the mistake of uttering an errant comment in passing. Often, disagreements and service related issues are created from passing comments in general that are taken at face value. Never tell a lie. If you don't tell one, you won't have to remember it. Many times, there may be a temptation to tell a "white lie" which seems innocent and non-threatening. Don't tell it. Don't embellish the facts or create stories. Just like lies, you won't have to remember them.

Honesty / Ethics

In a recent gallop poll, there was a question for those participating in the survey to rank the following professions for honesty and integrity. Car and life insurance sales professions ranked lowest in the poll while nurses and doctors ranked highest. There is a stigma that is attached to sales and sales people in general. I know many ethical professionals in both industries. Every effort is put forward to kill the negative stigma attached to those industries.

Here is another interesting statistic from that survey. Of all the participants who took that survey, nearly 85% of them viewed any sales profession in some negative way. We need to do all we can to ensure that we are demonstrating ethical behavior throughout the entire sales process. Ethical behavior is not a skill; it is a way of life.

As you gain experience in sales, you will gather many stories of your own – legitimate stories. Use those. If you don't have any, use someone else's stories as long as they are true. Never give someone the reason to question your ethics and honesty. This is very critical to establishing a solid relationship with your customer.

Passion

Imagine this. You are in the market for a television set. In today's Internet world, you are a well-educated consumer and thus have done your homework. Based on your research you know exactly the brand and model of television you are going to buy. Assume that you have to buy the television from a store. No matter what your choice of stores is, you will pay the same amount of money, to the penny. Also, this television set will be delivered from the same warehouse, by the same delivery people, at exactly the same time. There are absolutely no advantages purchasing from one store or another.

At the first store you go to, nobody says hello to you. You walk in the front doors and right to the large electronics section where it seems like a hundred televisions all playing the same channel, fill every inch of the store wall. Once in the electronics section, there are three reps talking in the corner. You stand in front of your new television set, admiring your new friend. Still nobody comes over to help you. After a few minutes, you leave. Nobody at the customer service counter acknowledges you or says goodbye to you as you leave the store. You feel disappointed and move on to the next store.

The second store is a much more pleasant experience. They pleasantly greet you as you walk in. You go to the electronics section and it has a similar display. This time, a sales agent greets you and excitedly you get into your dialogue about the set. Even though you have selected the television you want, the sales agent suggests comparable sets, which are on sale, and begins to print off slick sheets of 3 or 4 models. Politely you accept them and leave the store. You appreciate that the agent was looking out for your best interests and leave to review the information. The experience was a pleasant one.

The next day, you happen to drop into a third store. You encounter a greeting at the entrance and move yet again to the electronics section. You are greeted by a sales agent for the store. You explain your situation and what you're looking for. Immediately he begins to ask about your current stereo system, where the television is going to be and then asks you to draw a sketch on a scrap paper as to where the windows are in proximity to the television set. He compliments you on your system, your choice and then says, "if you don't purchase this television from me that's OK. I mean, I hope you do, but even if you find a better deal elsewhere and you need help setting it up, I will come over to your home and help you set it up."

Who would you give your sale to? More than likely, you would give your business to the person who became engaging and enthusiastic. In other words, you are more likely to consummate a business relationship with the person who is passionate about their product, service and industry. A little creative "value added proposition" helps tip the edge in favor of the last example.

Executives will tell you that they appreciate meeting with sales experts who demonstrate passion for what they do and the company that they represent.

Punctuality

Punctuality is another element that we demonstrate which really has no apparent value because it is a given that we show up on time for any scheduled meeting. Therefore, we really don't get bonus points for being on time.

However, if you are late for a scheduled meeting you immediately risk major points being deducted from your "likeability factor" grading system. The view from the customer's perspective, when you are late to your own meeting, is that the meeting is diminished in importance. You also run the risk of losing serious credibility and effectiveness with your customer if you are late.

The reality also stands true that sometimes, there are legitimate reasons beyond your control that can make you late for an appointment. Here's a little advice I learned early in my sales career. The one thing worse than being late, is being late and not calling. Everyone has a cell phone. In the rare event that your cell phone battery is dead, pull over and use the pay phone. If you don't

121

have a quarter, buy a calling card. There is no excuse for being late and not calling.

Here is the great benefit to calling your customer and re-establishing your credibility and trustworthiness. You will usually know if you are going to be late for an appointment well before the scheduled time. In that event, make the call. I would strongly recommend that if you are going to be so much as 1 minute late, pick up the phone and place that call.

The reality is this. If you call and your customer answers, you will be able to put your customer at ease with a brief explanation and you look credible, responsible and professional.

Many times however, you will get voice mail. At all cost you must leave a message. Here is why. Quite often the client is away from their desk when you arrive late for your meeting. You immediately apologize and ask if they received the message you left minutes ago. They will say no and tell you not to worry about it. They appease you and try to be a good host. In reality, you can be assured that after your meeting, your client will check to verify two things. One that you actually called and second that you called before your scheduled time.

Pay close attention to punctuality. Manage your time accordingly and leave a lot of time between calls so that you can arrive early.

Professionalism

During my sales training programs, participants are traditionally video taped at the beginning of the day during a role-play exercise. Client profiles are real examples. The application is specific to the company's products and services. The purpose of the exercise is two fold: identify areas of improvement in your presentation and further gain experience of what it is like from the other side of the desk – the customer's point of view.

These calls run at full length, just as long as a real first appointment would be, specific to that company's sales process. Once completed, the participants complete some keynotes and observations and as a group, we debrief the call.

During the debrief of the role play, it is fascinating to note that those in the sales rep role repeatedly score themselves well, feel that the call went very well while they look forward to the next step. In every role-play exercise that we have conducted, there is a very eye opening experience when the team playing the customer voices their opinion and shares their observations as to how they felt the call went.

On the surface, the feedback is cordial and generally complimentary. The selling team at a high level succeeds in demonstrating professionalism. This includes such things as being well dressed and groomed, enthusiastic and passionate. They demonstrated that they were well trained on their product knowledge.

But when the participants are asked to dig deep and peel back the onion, they begin to uncover skills such as questioning, listening and interpreting as being areas for improvement. Not being fully heard and the failure to create an impending moment for the next meeting are consistently echoed from program to program.

Summary

Sales experts will resist the urge to be overly friendly with their customer and thus maintain a level of seriousness and professionalism throughout the sales call. You must resist the urge to bring forward your solutions and talk about your products features and benefits. Give bits of information during your call and hold back the aces for your final presentation. This is how you can leave an impending moment so that your customer must see you for the next scheduled sales call.

This holds true with each selling situation. Being in the moment, undivided in your attention and genuinely interested in what the customer does is pinnacle in anchoring the relationship successfully.

Quite often, we fail to remember that although we may have presented and met with hundreds of customers in the past, asked the same questions and presented our value proposition repeatedly, the customer that you are seeing is meeting you for the first time. You and your information must remain fresh. Even if it is the second appointment, or the twenty-second appointment, be in the moment with your customer.

Don't forget that the approach you must take is that of wanting to help someone. Your whole objective is not to revolutionize the way the customer does their business, it's simply to help them do what it is that they do, a little better, faster, more simple, more effectively and more efficiently.

Selling should be simple. Your customer has to like you and trust you to help them do whatever it is that they do, a little bit better. The point is that if your customer manufactures soda pop today, you aren't going to suddenly get them to bottle milk tomorrow. It simply has to make sense for them to change or use your service, product or solution and empathy will go a long way to get you there.

Chapter Ten

Become *Exceptional* in Sales by Engaging Your Strengths and Managing Your Weaknesses

Being exceptional revolves around your strengths!

Take a look at your last evaluation. You and your sales manager probably made an action plan to make this year a better year than your last. Unfortunately, most of the action plans I have seen concentrate on the "needs improvement" list and pay little attention to the "exceeds expectations" list. Pause to think about this for a minute. If you really want to become exceptional, would it make more sense to try to fix your problem areas or engage your areas of strength? In which areas are you most likely to have an increase in sales? In which areas are you most likely to become *exceptional*?

Concentrating on fixing our weaknesses has been engrained in us almost from the crib. Our culture is set up to reward the underdog who has overcome obstacle after obstacle. So, when we have a weakness, we are asked to buckle down and practice, practice, practice until we can become competent.

We are told that.

OK, you just had your annual review. You made your numbers to stay out of trouble, but you didn't achieve your goals. You didn't make the income you had planned either. It was a good year, but not a great year. You want a great year!

After you attend the annual awards banquet you leave with the determination to make it into the winner's circle next year and you are frustrated because you didn't make it this year. In fact, you have been upset about not making it for the last three years. Why can't you break out of mediocre sales into exceptional sales? How do you go from being competent to exceptional? To begin with, stop trying to be well rounded and competent in all areas. This is not the road to success. Do you know what the definition of competent is? Adequate. Do you want to be adequate in sales? Adequate? What a horrible word! The adequate may wish to be exceptional someday, but the exceptional have never dreamed of being adequate.

Do you know someone like Jonathon Trysalot? Jonathon is one of those kids who have gone out for every sport under the sun. His parents understand that in order to get ahead in life one needs to be well rounded. So they sign Jonathon up for every opportunity to grow and nurture his natural talents. Unfortunately, no one can figure out Jonathon's natural talents because he is always so busy working on whatever skill is needed for the current day. He seemed to gravitate toward basketball. His dribbling skills came quickly and he was a pretty good shooter. Unfortunately, Jonathon never signed up for advanced basketball camp because it interfered with the start of soccer season, and well…Jonathon needs a lot more work on his soccer skills.

I'm not saying it isn't good to try new and different experiences. After all, we never know in what areas of life we can become exceptional unless we are exposed to them. However, we must stop trying to overcome all of our weaknesses in an effort to be well rounded.

Let's look at Jonathon again. If Jonathon's goal were to obtain a scholarship in sports and continue to participate during his college years, then what would be the best plan? Should Jonathon find as many sports as he can to be competent? In this case, competent would be defined as being able to make the first string and being a starter for the sport. Jonathon works hard to become good enough to start in three sports. He is competent in each. Do athletic scholarships go to the competent players or the exceptional players? Only the exceptional players are able to go on and compete at the college level. If Jonathon is serious about playing in college, he needs to become exceptional. Jonathon should build on his strengths. He should put his major efforts into the sport where his natural talents can be exploited. If Jonathon wants to play sports in college, he should concentrate on the sport in which he is most likely to become exceptional.

Key Question: Thinking back to when you were a child….as you went through school, do you remember being able to gravitate toward those classes where you could express your natural talents or were you consistently put into classes where you could work on your weaknesses? And then they wonder why students hate school. Shouldn't student's love school? Shouldn't they love to learn? The love of learning should be the top priority for our schools. Life long learning happens in those areas we love and which we can excel.

Engaging Your Strengths

Whenever you take a look at exceptional people, you find that they get to do what they do best everyday. They become the best because they have built upon their strengths. If you wish to be exceptional in sales, you need to find and build upon your strengths. You need to do what you do best every day. By doing what you do best, you can become the best in the world.

What do you do best? Many of us don't know what it is we do best. Many times we don't know our strengths. The first area in which you need to become an expert is in your strengths.

When discovering your strengths, you can consider listening to your inner voice. For years, your inner voice has pushed you toward those things you do best. What activities can you repeat almost perfectly? They involve your strengths. What skills come naturally to you and are easy to develop? They come from your strengths. By the influence of your inner voice you probably already have a belief that in order to get ahead in life you need to concentrate on what you do well and manage those things that you don't do so well. We all know this yet we spend most of our time trying to fix what is wrong!

In the past you have probably given more attention to areas of weaknesses than you have to your strengths in order to be well rounded. For this reason, like most people, it is hard for you to put into words what your strengths are. You haven't spent enough time getting to know your strengths. That is just what you need to do: spend *time* getting to know and developing your strengths.

Your goal is to become an expert in your strengths.

First, you need to start your Strengths Journal. You can buy a notebook and keep it on paper or build an electronic journal. Use the method that will be most comfortable to you. It should be easy and available for you to access. Listening to your inner voice, write down the answer to the following question:

What are your strengths and weaknesses?

This is a common question asked in a job interview. Visualize yourself interviewing for your current sales job or the sales job you wish to obtain. What clear and concise answer can you give the interviewer to show how your strengths will enable you to be *exceptional* in the sales position? Be sure to date this entry in your journal. As you discover and develop your strengths you will answer the question again and again.

Over time, your clear and concise answer to the interviewer's question will become truly remarkable. It will help you to obtain a laser-life focus on who you really are and what great value you bring to your employer. Your story will get better and better. Your ability to express your strengths will increase to the point where your future interviewers will know that you are truly exceptional.

You are learning to do what you do best.

A note on your weaknesses: you should concentrate only on those weaknesses that you will need to mange in order to be exceptional at the job you want. If your sales job requires you to "dress for success" but you are horrible at fashion, you will need to address that weakness and learn how to mange it. You could find someone who excels in the area of fashion and have her develop a wardrobe for you. You're not fixing your problem; you are working around it. You may never become an expert on fashion but you can still dress for success. Don't worry about your weaknesses that won't interfere with your drive to be exceptional. They don't matter.

You should now have a pretty good answer to the question "What are your strengths and weaknesses?" It will be interesting for you to see how your answer to this question evolves over time. You will be surprised at how quickly your answer becomes truly remarkable.

Another exercise to discover your strengths and weaknesses is for you to be the interviewer. Sit down with a friend, colleague, your boss, your spouse…anyone who knows you well. Ask them to answer the question, "What are my strengths and weaknesses?"

NOTE: You have to be thick-skinned. You are asking these folks for their help and for their honest opinion. You are obligated to treat their answers with respect. If their opinion doesn't sit well with you, don't react. Take it home with you and read it over in a calm moment. Their insight could be a great blessing. It might just help you engage your strengths faster than anything else. We all love hearing how wonderful our strengths are, but we also need to face the brutal facts of our weaknesses.

Enter the interviews into your strengths log. Read the interviews and ponder the strengths others have noticed in you. Then, re-write your answer to the question, "What are your strengths and weaknesses?" You will notice an evolution to the remarkable starting to blossom. It will excite you because you are moving toward the real you.

OK, you have written your answers as if you were in a job interview. You have been the interviewer and asked a few friends to list your strengths. You have then pondered the results and re-written your answers. Now you should do some more research. I love living in the age of technology! Go back to your search engine. This is where you put your time into becoming an expert in your strengths. No one becomes an expert in anything overnight.

You and I engage our strengths so that we can do what we do best everyday. By engaging your strengths you will be able to do what you do best everyday. This is what gives you a chance to become exceptional! You can be the best in the world but only in the areas of your strengths. So start engaging your strengths.

You should always return to your Strengths Journal. Whenever you read a book, put your notes in your journal. After you take any assessment, put your notes in your journal. When you visit a website, have your journal available to take notes. This will give you a convenient place where you can access all your research on your strengths.

In the back of your journal I want you to make a section entitled "Inspired Action". In order to move forward to becoming exceptional in sales, you have to take action. You need to take some action toward becoming exceptional everyday. Keep your list of actions in your "Inspired Action" section of your journal.

When you start your research, you will be inspired to take action. We all get moments of inspiration. Thoughts about something we need to do to make our lives better. The problem is that we don't write them down and we soon forget them. We can't move closer to engaging our strengths without taking action.

I get my inspired thoughts for action at many different times during the day. When I'm doing my research and taking notes I often feel impressed to take some kind of action. I open my "Inspired Action" log and write down my thoughts. Then at night, when I am writing down my schedule for the next day, I review my list and decide which action steps I need to take. This process ensures me that I will have plenty of inspired actions to take each day.

You will be inspired at different times in your day. Someone you talk to may say something that sparks an idea. Write it down! When you read a book or do research on the web, thoughts for action will come to you. Write it down! Perhaps as you are doing your exercise routine an idea will come to you. Write it down! Some of my best ideas come to me during my morning run. Inspirational moments such as these are powerful. You should keep your mind open to any new idea that may come. Besides those random moments when you pick up an idea here and there, you may want to dedicate time each day to meditation and contemplation during which you can ponder the things you are working on. This time will become sacred to you. You will find that taking time out of your day to ponder the things that are important to you will enable you to attack your remaining time with enthusiasm. We all need to have a time where we can express our gratitude for all the opportunities in our life.

Start your research today. Discover your strengths and engage them in your sales process. Become the best at what you do. You are on a journey to become exceptional.

Manage Your Weaknesses

We all have weaknesses and we should make an effort to find out what weaknesses could slow us down in our quest to become exceptional. However, we can't make it our life's pursuit to fix all our problem areas, because focusing on weakness has never made anyone exceptional.

There are some weaknesses that can cripple you in sales. If you are a weak communicator, it will be very difficult to become exceptional in sales. You have to be able to communicate to your customers. If you are determined to be exceptional in sales, you will have to develop strong communication skills. As you practice these skills, learn how you can use your strengths to make up for your weakness.

Developing a strong reputation for after-sales service could offset your weakness. Your clients will buy from you despite your weakness because they know your reputation for service.

I know a lady who has little empathy. Whenever her clients complain to her of their problems, she often can't relate and so she determines in her mind that they are minor and will ignore them. This causes larger problems down the road, which translates into loss of sales. In order to manage her weakness, she has trained herself to always ask the following question at the end of every client interaction, "Now, are there any problems I need to address before our next meeting?" As her clients answer this question, it gives her feedback to problems that she may not have picked up on due to her poor empathy skills.

I know another sales rep that is as random as they come. His dress and paper work are often a mess. He forgets to return phone calls. He appears to his clients to be totally disorganized. His sales suffered because no one wanted to trust their assets with someone who is so unstructured. This was a big weakness for him to overcome. He made some progress by taking a time management class and cleaning up his office, but he just couldn't keep from falling back into old habits. I suggested that he go out and find the most detail-oriented assistant he could find to keep him on track.

It worked out wonderfully. He hired an assistant that kept his office area clean and organized, scheduled his appointments, made reminder and follow-up phone calls and chased down problems. This created a reputation for him as being totally organized! He managed his weakness by teaming up with someone who had the organizational skills he lacked. Who's on your team? Do they complement you or are they just like you? Which would make more sense?

Managing your weaknesses isn't about ignoring them. Sometimes we have to take training to become competent enough in a needed skill. The point isn't to ignore, but to realize that we do not become exceptional by improving our weaknesses. We may be competent, but not exceptional. We become exceptional by engaging our strengths!

A Call to Action

Start your journal today and keep adding to it until you can answer the question, "What are your strengths?" with an absolutely remarkable answer! By learning your strengths, you will become a more authentic person. You will "walk the talk." It will be exciting because you have engaged your strengths in the sales process. You will love getting up in the morning and going to work. Work will become more fun. The best part is that you will be on your way to becoming truly *exceptional!*

Chapter Eleven

The Power of Sales Strategies, Processes and Routines

[Ed. Note- Corporate Athletes, take note! Nobody knows performance strategies and routines like Dr. Mollie Marti. Using the innovative tools shared in the next few chapters will quickly take your performance to the next level.]

Successful sales professionals incorporate strategies and routines into their daily life. Strategies and routines work together to engage your mind and body to perform the task at hand. In short, *strategies* are processes designed to achieve desired outcomes. *Routines* are patterns of thinking and acting that engage your mind and body in a way that increases your ability to appropriately respond to stress. Routines help keep you on track and protect you from outside influences so that you can perform your strategies.

Prospective Approach

Strategies and routines are an inherent part of a *prospective*, or forward looking, approach to sales performance. A prospective approach defines performance as the capacity and freedom to *choose* your level of performance each and every day. How is this accomplished? By focusing on the process rather than just the outcomes.

When you take a prospective approach, your dream about winning that top sales award is not limited to standing at the podium receiving the plaque. The dream from a prospective standpoint is living the process of earning it. You see yourself meeting larger clients, making the sales, getting more referrals, and growing your business to a more profitable level.

Talk to some top award winners in your industry. You will hear few details about the day they received an award or the moment they reached a certain level of production. Rather, you will hear story after story as they relive the process leading up to the recognition. They remember details of preparation, meeting clients for the first time, making the perfect presentation, identifying and meeting the needs of clients, landing a big client, and building relationships

131

with mentors and colleagues. They can see themselves in the midst of their growth and remember the feelings of satisfaction. They can tell stories about the process all day long.

Retrospective Approach

A retrospective, or backward looking, approach to sales, on the other hand, focuses on the outcomes. Did you make the sale – or not? This focus on the outcomes leads to a determination to get the sale at any cost, working harder without reason, hammering away without an end in sight and working out of fear.

These types of behaviors might be seen as virtuous to some of you reading this book. It is counterintuitive to say don't focus on the results, given that the goal of sales is to produce results. Yet, a prospective approach to sales shares this goal of producing outcomes. You need certain outcomes in production and meeting quotas and closing a high number of sales are crucial to success. The key to understanding a prospective approach to sales is appreciating that *when you focus on the process, the outcomes not only follow, they significantly increase.*

To better understand the power of a prospective approach to sales, let's look at the downsides of using a retrospective approach. When you measure your success by your outcomes, you lack valid information that could be used to improve your sales performance. Information about the sales process is quickly lost without a system in place to capture it. By the time you have finished a project or made (or lost) a sale, you have already forgotten more than you accurately recall about your performance. So you use your end results as a determination of how you did . . . or start looking around at how others did.

A readily available outcome standard is the performance of others. Measuring your outcomes against the outcomes of people around you is a type of social comparison. These comparisons abound in the sales area. How is your level of production, compared to others in your company or within your industry? This comparison can be deceiving and de-motivating.

If you happen to perform better than others, you might be tempted to look at others and think, "Hey, I'm doing pretty good. I'd like to see you sell at my level." Or, "I have only been here three years and my numbers are better than Joe's and he's been here ten years. Good for me." You are mistaken if you use such comparisons. So what if your numbers are better than every one else in your company? Isn't the real question, how are you performing? Are you performing at your optimal level?

The effect on your motivation can be even more detrimental when you make comparisons to those whose outcomes are better than yours. At one extreme, you might intentionally compare yourself to those who are doing better in order to make your self-view more positive. You compare yourself to elite sales professionals and search for similarities in order to convince yourself that you are doing great.

At the other extreme, you might compare yourself to those who are selling at a higher level and use the information as confirmation of how poorly you are doing. This will completely sap your motivation. You will get beat up emotionally and run the risk of thinking, "Why do I even try? I'll never get there." Every task looks much more difficult than it looked before you filled your head with these comparisons. When you go to make your next sales call, that 1-pound telephone just became a 100-pound telephone.

The real question is how are *you* performing? Are you performing at your best possible level? Imagine that you just made the best sales presentation you were capable of making that day, but did not make the sale. Using a retrospective approach, you fell short. You lost the sale. End of story. Better luck next time – and good luck getting motivated for your next attempt. This same experience, when viewed prospectively, has the potential to fire you up. You know that you did your best under the circumstances, you have the tools to analyze how and why you fell short, you put a plan in place to make the necessary changes, and you are motivated to work even harder to take your sales performance to the next level.

Social comparisons, whether to those who are doing better than you or to those who are doing worse, have a wide range of effects. Yes, some of these comparisons can help you feel better. For example, you might tend to look for someone else who has it worse. You compare yourself to those who are sicker, less fortunate, work harder or make less money and this makes you feel better about your situation. When it comes to your sales performance, however, comparisons to others can quickly undermine your motivation level and performance. From here on out, limit your comparisons to within yourself. The questions to ask are: "How am I performing?" "Am I performing at my best level?" "Am I improving every day?"

My years of consulting in the human performance field have confirmed that a retrospective approach is the wrong approach to staying motivated and selling at a consistently high level over time. When you put a process in place and continue to hone the execution of that process, you minimize mistakes and missed opportunities. What does this mean in your world of sales? It could mean that by focusing on the process, you begin to minimize the times you make any of the following common sales mistakes: making a poor first impression, asking the wrong question, asking the right question at the wrong time, failing to return telephone calls on time, failing to follow up when a prospective client says they need some time to think things over, overlooking the small details, over promising and under delivering, or failing to ask for referrals. This list scratches the surface. We could generate a long list of possible mistakes and missed opportunities for your profession that ultimately results in decreased sales.

Not only will focusing on the process help you to minimize mistakes, but it also will directly improve your performance. It will lead to increased networking, more and better contacts, higher quality appointments, a higher closing ratio, and greater sales. It puts you in the best possible position to generate high quality leads, turn those leads into prospects, turn those prospects into clients, and turn those clients into life-long raving fans who generate even more business for you through their high-quality referrals.

How many times have you heard someone comment, "That guy gets all the breaks"? Do not buy it. Those "lucky" people "get the breaks" because they put themselves in a position to see opportunities and seize them. This wisdom is not new. "Luck is when preparation meets opportunity," stated Seneca, a first century philosopher. This is why it is so important to use a proactive system to capture information about mistakes you make in the sales process. You can then fully prepare for the next appointment by using this information to build strategies to remedy these mistakes. If you do not have a system in place to ensure progressive growth, you will close sales on an inconsistent basis and, eventually at a lower level. How frustrating it becomes when you cannot figure out how you hit your target one day, but missed it by a long shot the next. This inconsistency and repeatedly letting opportunities slip through your fingers will prevent you from experiencing the potential for fun and fulfillment provided by a career in sales.

When you proactively build and use sales strategies, you think about what you are doing as you do it. This keeps you focused on the relevant information in your environment so you will be less likely to make mistakes and more likely to perform well on a consistent basis. This process also allows you to more accurately recount what you did during a sales performance. This information can then be used to learn, make necessary adjustments in your strategies, and take your performance to an even higher level. Let's take a more detailed look at exactly what strategies are, why they are effective, and the keys to building and using them to unleash your sales power.

Strategies

Strategies are processes designed to achieve your desired outcome. The value of a strategy is it allows you to maintain a process-oriented focus and channel your efforts toward achieving your objectives. With a properly executed strategy, you do not get pulled out of the process by the perceived demands of the intended results ("I *have* to make this sale") or by other irrelevant distractions. Remember the dangers of social comparisons that were discussed earlier? A strategy also ensures that you employ the best possible tactics for your performance instead of trying to perform according to someone else's standards.

Your strategy will provide a *consistent* level of performance. When you construct an effective strategy and properly execute it, it will provide a baseline level of performance. Some days (ideally, most days), you will outperform this basic level. You might be thinking, "Aren't you forgetting about the prospective client? He's the one holding the cards. He might be having a bad day, or he is defensive, or he doesn't really get what I am trying to sell, or he just doesn't like my shirt. How can I consistently make sales when people can be so fickle? " A strategy for a specific sales task will use the same process again and again. Sales are about numbers and we know that not everyone will buy. But if your process is built in a way that genuinely introduces you and your product, makes the prospective client feel understood and appreciated, builds trust, and tailors the value of the product to the prospective client's needs and unique situation, then it will consistently lead to sales. At a minimum, this process will establish the basis for a future relationship with the prospective client. When you truly understand the consistency that strategies provide, you will be in a position to unleash the full power of building and using sales strategies.

Your sales strategies are unique to you and the present task. Well-constructed strategies take into consideration your current mental and physical dispositions, skill level, and performance capabilities. They include accountability, are positive, and are progressively ordered. For example, in sales there is an ideal sequencing of steps. Your strategies must take this sequencing into account because even if you perform the correct steps, you can still lose a sale if you do not perform them in the correct order. Finally, well-constructed strategies get you in the proper mindset for accomplishing the task at hand and help you channel your full attention to the right things at the right time.

At the most basic level, strategies can be broken down into four types of cues or triggers: mechanical, mental, physical, and performance. To better understand these types of triggers, let's use a sports analogy of running as an additional application.

Mechanical Triggers

Mechanical triggers, which are sometimes called instructional cues, provide the essential "how to" information. In sales, this information is needed in order to know how to generate leads, how to greet a prospect, how to conduct a prospective client interview, how to close a sale, and how to ask for a referral.

Mechanical triggers take into account that the process changes as you proceed through different phases of a sale. They often include mental and physical aspects, which are discussed in more detail below. The equivalent triggers for a runner would include how to start, how to position their body, how to lean on the turn, when they need to steadily cruise, and when they need to kick it into higher gear.

This type of expertise in sales often rests with your manager or training department. In an ideal world, your company has a process in place to progressively train salespeople in the sales strategies that have been shown most effective for their products. Unfortunately, this can be the exception rather than the rule.

Lacking a real understanding of the essential steps to effectively sell one's product is not limited to newer sales professionals. I have met countless sales professionals who have been in sales for years and have never been walked through the ideal sales process for their product. If you do not have training resources available within your company, invest in a mentor or coach to help you construct proper mechanical triggers. With great diligence on your part, this information also can be gleaned from books or audio resources that include specific knowledge of your sales arena.

Mental Triggers

Mental triggers identify the places within the overall strategy that trigger the next part of the strategy. It is like flipping a card. This cue marks a point where you forget what is behind you and refocus on the current place.

As a mental cue, runners would mark some part of the race (a distance, a turn, a point in the course) to trigger the next part of the race strategy. This would differ between a short-range race and a long-mileage race. A marathoner might identify a different mental cue for the start than for the first ten miles, the next ten miles, and the final six miles.

Mental triggers help you create a shortcut in your mind. Psychologists call these *heuristics*. These shortcuts serve as highly effective ways to make rapid decisions and judgments, even when under stress or time constraints. Boiling down all the complexities of performing a task to concise steps keeps you from overloading your mind with all of the details every time you perform a familiar task.

Mark the important mental triggers in your sales process. Perhaps you greet the prospective client by asking them a few personal questions about their family, work and interests. You finish this initial dialogue. Mental cue flips. Your introduction is behind you and you now focus on the next step. This might be a series of questions to find out why your product is important to them and what needs or desires it fulfills. It might be a series of questions about the prospective client's best and worst buying experiences or their desired level of involvement in the sales process. Another mental cue would flip you into your closing questions.

Physical Triggers

You may associate physical triggers more strongly with athletics than with sales. When elite athletes push their bodies to the high level that is needed for competition, they are going to experience physical sensations. A runner would build physical triggers into his strategy to tell himself what his body will be experiencing at different points of the race so he can prepare for it. This will help keep the physical demands from taking him out of his race.

Do not fool yourself into thinking that your sales position does not involve physical aspects. Managing your physical energy is an important part of being successful in sales. Similar to the demands of a competitive athlete, sales professionals need to train like corporate athletes. A high level of stamina is needed to manage the complexity and volume of information processed daily in a sales profession. Without a high level of stamina, just thinking about the ever-changing technological systems, competitive pressures, long hours, travel demands, and need to do more with less can make you tired. Business professionals will realize great benefits from defining themselves as corporate athletes, training like athletes, and using competitive strategies on a daily basis.

You also have a unique personality and physiology that interacts with your work demands to produce a physical effect. You need to become familiar with your body and how it functions in different situations so you can work with your tendencies to perform at your best level. Perhaps you tend to become anxious in social settings or when speaking to a group of people. When this anxiety becomes apparent to others, especially when meeting a prospective client for the first time, it can give the wrong message. For example, the other person might think that you are getting caught up in yourself because you are sending the message that you are worried about how you are being perceived. If this is the case, you are skewing the sales process to become focused on yourself. This is completely at odds with how clients view the process, and rightly so. You are not selling. The client is buying. The focus needs to move from "I wonder what they are thinking about me" and "I wonder what I'm doing wrong" to "What does my client need?" and "How can I and my product give them more of what they need?" You can quickly lose a sale when a client senses that you think your interaction is about you and not them.

Managing your physical sensations is an area of sales where you might need to "fake it until you make it" while you change some deeply ingrained thoughts. Become familiar with your body and how it performs throughout the sales process. Understand that these sensations are normal for you. Learn to work with them instead of fighting them. You might need to build some long-term strategies to change deeply ingrained negative self-perceptions and self-talk. In the meantime, utilize on demand techniques to appear calm and confident even when your heart feels like it is going to pound out of your chest.

Building physical triggers into your sales strategies can help you more quickly move from faking it, which requires an immense amount of energy, to truly being comfortable with how you function throughout the whole sales process.

A discussion of the physical elements of sales would not be complete without emphasizing the importance of nonverbal physical cues. A successful sales professional must have a thorough grasp of reading and responding to nonverbal cues. When your clients are leaning forward or nodding their head, you might continue with one strategy. If they sit back in their chair, cross their arms, or give "that look" to their partner, you need to process this information as it happens and quickly kick into an alternative strategy.

Performance Triggers

Performance triggers or markers involve using the performance of competitors as benchmarks for your performance. Knowing when and how your performance stacks up against others can provide information about the need for and timing of executing alternative strategies.

Elite runners need a thorough understanding of how they stand in comparison to their competitors. If a certain competitor is quickly gaining on them or has taken the lead, it is time to kick in an alternative strategy. A highly proficient salesperson is also capable of using this type of information. If you are one of several salespeople making a proposal to a large prospective client, you might want to use performance triggers in your sales strategies.

I strongly advise less experienced salespeople, however, to avoid using this type of comparative information. Remember the "no social comparisons" rule from earlier in this chapter? When we use others to judge ourselves, we set ourselves up for performance errors and decreased motivation. For many salespeople, the best performance cue is to build in assessment points when you ask, "Am I performing at the level I know how to perform?" and "Am I fully executing my strategy?"

Information that every sales person should be looking for, recording, and utilizing is information provided by their prospective clients. If you are preparing to prospect a corporation, gain a thorough understanding of their culture. Use information gathered in each meeting with a prospective client to fully prepare for the next meeting. Preparation for a left-brain, highly detailed client should differ from follow-up with a right brain, big picture client. Follow-up with a highly conscientious personality would be more particular than follow-up with a more laid back client. Does the person sitting across from you have a high or low tolerance for risk? Are they extroverted or introverted? Is their family most important to them or are they driven by a strong ego of self and their own success? Where are they in the sales process?

To be successful, your appointment preparation and interaction must be tailored to your prospective client's personality, preferences, and present status.

Relate this to how an elite runner needs to become familiar with the hills, hallows and lonely stretches of the racecourse. This information enables him to respond to the unique demands by, for example, preparing to run hills differently than running the flats. By anticipating the specific challenges of the terrain and employing the correct strategy in training and competition, the runner will conserve energy and maximize performance. Similarly, when you incorporate unique information about your prospective client into your strategies in a spirit of fully understanding them and responding to who they are and what they need, you go well beyond simply trying to make a sale. Of course, these outcomes naturally follow when you put the correct process into place.

Strategy Construction

Remember that at the heart of a prospective approach to performance is the concept that if you *focus on the process*, the outcomes will follow. You can now see how strategies provide the processes to achieve your goals. They include the mechanics or the "how to" perform your task. You gather information to answer essential questions in your field of sales. For example, what is the best way for you to identify where people are in the buying cycle? What is the best system to capture this information? What are the best methods to follow up at the appropriate time? You then use the answers to these types of questions as the meat of your sales strategies. Strategies organize this information into a usable process.

When you build a sales strategy for a particular task, take into consideration your current mental and physical dispositions. For example, when you become self-conscious, do you tend to shut down or do you incessantly babble? Also take into account your skill level and performance capabilities. A strategy for a starting sales person who has a minimal level of familiarity with a line of products would look different than a strategy for an experienced sales person who knows all of their products inside and out.

Give careful thought to progressively ordering your strategy. In sales there is an ideal sequencing of steps. Your strategies must take this sequencing into account because even if you perform the correct steps, you can still lose a sale if you do not perform them in the correct order. Structure your strategies to get you emotionally fired up to accomplish the task at hand and to channel your full attention to the right things at the right time.

When you are first developing a strategy for a sales task, I strongly recommend that you write out all four types of triggers (mechanical, mental, physical and performance) in preparation for your performance. Design in detail how the task would be performed if you did everything right. You can build strategies for your first meeting with a prospective client, making a sales presentation, closing a sale, conducting a client review appointment, asking for

139

a referral, and each of your other sales tasks. When you first write these out, make them as detailed as possible. Write them so that someone who knows nothing about sales or the task that you are performing could get a clear picture in their head about the actions they would need to take to successfully perform the task.

After you have written out a complete and detailed strategy for your task, go through and underline the key action steps. Begin to boil down these actions to a specific word or simple term in your mind. These powerful heuristics or short-cut reminders are what you want in your mind as you perform the task in front of you. I have seen top performers, when executing a new strategy, say or whisper these words out loud. In an athletic event, it might be, "power," "lean," "lift." In a sales event, it might be, "smile," listen," "posture." This is a good way to keep a strategy in your head and speed up the process of making the strategy part of your automatic processing.

Place subtle reminders in your environment to help you remember your strategy until it becomes an automatic process. This takes me back to my early years of marriage when my husband, who is now a wealth manager, would walk around the house repeatedly whispering the word "fact" while mentally preparing for an appointment. It made me question his sanity until I realized what he was doing. He was just starting out in the financial industry with a career in insurance and one of his managers had taught him to use mnemonics or memory aids in the sales process. The FACT mnemonic was used when meeting a prospective client for the first time. FACT was to remind him to ask questions about the person's Family, Activities, Career and Time. These represented questions about a person's family and relationships, hobbies they enjoyed, their work and career aspirations, and how they valued spending time, such as what community or volunteer work was important to them. These are all non-threatening areas that people enjoy talking about while providing a sales person with some insight into the needs and desires of the other person. He was given different mnemonics to use when gathering asset information or conducting other parts of the sales process. These aids served as important guidelines for my husband as he started his career in sales. My husband's potential clients would not notice a small "FACT" written at the top of his intake sheet, but they would notice that the man in front of them was showing a genuine interest in them and their life.

Summary

Think about your general standards for measuring your performance. Are you highly focused on outcomes? Do you find yourself comparing your performance to others? Do you spend valuable time and energy recovering from a disappointing outcome? Is your performance inconsistent and you don't know why? If the answer to any of these questions is yes, then you can improve your performance by building and using effective sales strategies. Your strategies will work hand in hand with the clear, authentic, energizing value-based life direction that you learned how to build earlier in this book.

This book could not possibly provide all of the strategies you need in your sales profession because strategies are *unique* to you. This book does provide extensive information about the importance, purpose, components, and execution of strategies. It also is full of rich examples of effective strategies used by successful people in the sales industry. Sit down with your mentor, your manager, or a coach to individualize this information to your sales practice and build your ideal sales strategies.

When you successfully execute a solid strategy, it will provide a consistent level of high performance. As mentioned at the beginning of this chapter, a necessary component of using your strategies is building a routine. Routines buffer you from all of those things going on in your work environment. As you know, information continually comes at you from all different directions and distractions threaten to throw you off course. This is where a routine comes in. You now understand how to use a strategy to take you from the start of a sales task to the completion of it. As discussed in the following chapter, using routines beyond these points ensures that you get your strategy in your head and stay on task during your performance.

Chapter Twelve

Routines: Rituals of Achievement

[Ed. Note- Rituals are those behaviors we all do that bring us a sense of comfort and familiarity. Christmas, taking a few swings at the plate before standing in the batter's box...Dr. Marti shows you how to use rituals to achieve. K.H.]

With the complexity of your business and the sales process itself, there are a million things going on in your environment to pull you away from the task at hand. Your daily life is crammed full of "to do" actions and distractions. Say you do the work suggested in the last chapter and develop strategies for prospecting, presenting, responding to objections, closing and other aspects of your sales process. But how can you keep these sales strategies in your head? This is when you need to use routines.

A routine is a recognized and disciplined pattern of behavior that engages your mind, body and emotions. It is designed to reduce *unfamiliarity, unpredictability* and *lack of control*. These are three of the biggest factors that erode or detract from your performance. These factors can quickly decrease the amount of mental capacity available to take in, process and recall information. They also decrease your ability to focus on the relevant cues in a situation. It's not that you don't want to give your full attention; it just becomes too difficult when there is so much going on around you. Sometimes the loudest noise is coming from within your own head. Negative expectations, doubts, fears, anxiety and self-questioning can quickly undermine your performance.

Routines decrease feelings of unfamiliarity by preparing you ahead of time for your performance. When you have already seen yourself performing in your mind, it becomes easier to repeat this performance in your external world. Routines also decrease unpredictability by providing structure and consistency. They put you in control of your situation by fully preparing you to execute your strategy and keeping you on task.

Routines regulate your behavior and engage your optimal mental, physical and emotional states. They engage your mind so you best take in and process all of the complex information in front of you. They help focus your attention to the relevant cues and block out all distractions. They help get you in a position so that you are pumped up and ready to perform the task at hand. They

143

energize you, increasing your confidence that you can perform a task. Routines also ensure that you recoup energy during your day. This is essential when you are in a long meeting or are performing several tasks at a continuous high level over a long period of time. Routines allow you to rest before hand but when it's time to perform . . . boom! You are ready for it.

You need to practice your routines until they become second nature. This means that if you get away from your routine, it will throw you off. It just won't feel right. This is a good thing because it means that when you use your routines, they will provide consistency. When you harness the power of routines, you can start to *choose* your level of performance. Does this mean that you'll set a new and higher level of sales every day from then on? Not quite. You are not likely to have the best performance of your life when you have the flu or were awaken 3 times the night before by a sick child. Can you still wake up every day and make conscious choices and take specific actions to choose to perform at the highest level available to you on that day? Yes!

Routines can be grouped into three general types: preparation, pre-event and post-event. Preparation and pre-event routines are similar. You want them to be. When you have a competitive event, such as a corporate sales proposal, you can use a preparation routine daily as you practice for the proposal. This ensures that when you go to make your proposal, your body is trained. On the day of your proposal, you would use your same preparation routine to get ready to go. More immediate to the proposal, you might use a separate pre-event routine. Finally, after every event, you would use a post-event routine. This is especially important when you are performing multiple events. You need to get rid of any negative emotions generated by your past performance and then fully prepare for your next event.

My research has identified ten separate components of routines. All of these components will be introduced here, with greater attention given to those used most frequently in sales. The components are: an expectancy to perform, an appropriate rest cycle, influence management, mental priming, physical priming, emotional priming, focal point establishment, performance rehearsal, engagement cue and strategy review. Your routines will be unique to you and structured in a way that works best for you. There is no required order to these components with a few exceptions. As discussed below, the engagement cue is the very last thing you do immediately before a performance. Also, the strategy review belongs in your post-event routine.

Components of Routines:

Now let's take a closer look at the different components of a routine.

1. Expectancy to Perform

As you begin preparing for a performance, consciously make a choice to expect good things to happen. Think and say, "I expect to perform". Write this expectation out and keep it in from of you. This positive expectation provides a mental framework for your performance. William James, the noted early American psychologist, said, "It is our attitude at the beginning of a difficult task which, more than anything else, will affect its successful outcome."

Successful sales professionals understand that a task itself is neutral. It is the performer who brings emotion to the task. These emotions can seem to saturate the task and create the sense that it is the task itself that is so big, demanding or emotionally charged. That telephone only feels like it weighs one hundred pounds when a sales professional looks at it and thinks, "Man, I hate cold calling. How much rejection can a person take?" Another sales professional could look at that same telephone and think, "Great, I get to make calls for the next hour! I love talking to new people and taking on the challenge of introducing my great products and myself. I am not only going to feel a sense of accomplish after working through this list of contacts, but I also am giving others an opportunity to benefit from a wonderful product that is going to improve their lives."

On a broader level, adopt a positive expectancy to perform your best, each and every day. "This is what I am going to do today. I am going to perform at my best." So many times we forget that we have the freedom to make this choice. We wake up and the first thought might be, "It's too early," "I hate that alarm clock," or "Great . . . another day of sameness." Or perhaps you wait to look out the window and let the weather determine your mood. "Yuck. It's gray and cloudy. It's going to be a gloomy, boring day." Make a choice to expect positive results, each and every day.

2. Rest Cycle

Think about the amount of energy you pour out within a single day. You expend mental, physical and emotional energy on a variety of tasks from the minute you wake up in the morning until your head hits the pillow at night. You give energy away through the telephone, other people, your car, your computer and countless other interactions. As you expend energy during the day, you need to build in ways to recoup the expended energy. You do this by incorporating rest cycles into your day.

Rest is any activity, in and of itself, which is pleasurable and restorative. What is restful to you might not be to another person. You know what types of activities refuel and energize you. In order to perform at your optimal level, you need to build these fun activities into each day. It does not work to bust it all week and think that you will rejuvenate on the weekend.

Energy management is so essential to performing at a high level, that it is given greater attention in a later chapter. The important point for establishing routines is that you need to build in rest cycles that are appropriate to the stress you have experienced leading up to your performance. After a 30-minute staff meeting, this might involve chatting with a co-worker for a few minutes on the way back to your desk. After working at your computer for an hour, it might be sufficient to stand up and stretch for a couple of minutes before switching to your next activity. After a two-hour sales meeting, rest might involve getting a drink of water or a small snack to refuel or taking a quick walk around the block. After a hectic morning of unexpected or demanding telephone calls, you might want to close your eyes for a few minutes and focus on restoring your energy with rhythmic breathing.

Do what you need to do to refuel and recharge before every performance. Make a conscious choice to fill up your gas tank. If you do not build this in as you prepare for a performance, you will not have an optimal level of energy available to you to draw upon when you need it.

3. Influence Management

Before any performance, you need to clear your mind so you can focus on the task at hand. How many times have you been trying to focus on an important task while your mind has been pulled away to something else? Often times it is an emotionally charged issue that pulls your mind away. You are carrying emotions from an unresolved issue that continues to eat away at you.

What do you do if you are carrying negative emotions? You are nervous, fearful, frustrated, anxious, angry, tired or feeling guilty. These emotions will pull you away from your strategies. When you wallow in negative emotions, you take precious energy away from the situation in front of you. In sales, when you are frequently interacting with others, this will result in making a lesser contribution. This will not help you or your clients.

Try a technique called *pitching* to help discharge negative emotions on demand. Pitching means identifying a specific negative emotion, linking it with a physical action and discarding it. The idea is to grab the emotion and throw it out of your head. Your pitching action has to be *unique* in order to tell your mind that you are taking control.

I recommend beginning with a basic pitching image of a backpack. Name your emotion and see it as a heavy rock sitting in your backpack, weighing you down. Physically reach back into your backpack, pick up the emotion, identify it and throw it. Visualize the rock flying through the air, crashing to the ground and breaking into hundreds of tiny pieces. When you first start to pitch, try to physically perform these actions, which will give your mind a strong sign that, "I am taking control!" As you practice this tool, you are going to get so good at discharging emotion that you can do it all in your head simply by choosing to "pitch it." Negative emotion gone. Back to your strategy.

146

Pitching is an extremely effective method of discharging negative emotion on demand. Think about the competitive edge this tool provides. While your competitor is distracted and still fuming over the fight he had with his wife this morning, you are fully focused on your big sales proposal. Do not forget that if there is a larger unresolved problem, it will still be there after you have completed your presentation, sales appointment or meeting. The sooner you build a strategy to manage this underlying energy-draining issue, the sooner you will experience a higher level of energy to give to other important tasks.

4. Mental Priming

You need to warm up your brain in preparation to perform at your highest level. It is important to do this ahead of time so that you do not waste time during the performance itself waiting for your brain to warm up. Your brain is an amazing machine. When you prime one node or pattern of thought, it trickles down to many related thoughts. All you have to do is prime the pump.

An essential part of mental priming is reviewing your strategy execution. This requires that you have your strategies in place. Perhaps you start by writing out your presentation in full. As you practice it, you work off of a concise outline. You never give the exact same presentation but you have a clear structure and flow. In preparation for your performance, mentally review your strategy execution. See your performance play out in your mind. Think through it in detail, "I will do this, I will be thinking this, I will be looking for this, I should be feeling this." End with a statement that you are mentally ready for the challenge.

Advanced and complex software packages and video simulations are available to warm up a performer's brain. There is support for the effectiveness of these activities. For example, a recent study found that surgeons who played certain non-violent video games at least a few hours each week made significantly fewer errors and performed faster than their non-gaming colleagues. These games improved skills used in surgery including motor skills, reaction time and hand-eye coordination. This type of stimulation is not limited to the use of technology. Prior to your performance, exercise your brain with a puzzle, read a thought provoking article, or spend ten minutes doing all activities with your non-dominant hand. Look out the window, identify all of the various colors and hues present in the view, and then narrow your focus down to study the intricacies of a single color. The methods of waking up your brain are endless.

We operate in a complex world filled with distractions and potential misunderstandings. A wide-awake brain can better scan the environment, take in relevant cues, block out distractions and recall important information. It can better read your client's nonverbal behavior, process data and more quickly generate higher quality solutions. It will facilitate communication with clients, co-workers and others. Make sure to wake up your brain before every performance so when it is time to perform, all you need to do is flip the switch.

5. Physical priming

You need to physically prime your body to perform at its optimal level. Get it physically warmed up so it is ready to go when you tell it to turn it on. Do not fool yourself into thinking that you sit in an office much of the day so there are no real physical demands to your job. Without a conscious choice to stretch and physically warm up your body, you will give a flat, ho-hum performance. Do not waste the precious first moments of a performance warming up your body to the necessary level. You will lose a client's attention with such a slow start or give a sub par performance because you never properly engaged your body.

Remember the law of conservation that you learned about in an earlier chapter? Your body abides by this law and will only produce as much energy as necessary to get the job done. If you do not get your heart pumping, you increase the possibility that your mind will assess the task as too easy and so not provide enough energy for an optimal performance.

Ideally, you want to spike or rapidly increase your heart rate a couple of times as you prepare for any big performance. If you are familiar with your maximum heart rate (the maximum heart rate that you should achieve during maximal physical exertion), aim for reaching 60-70% of this rate at least once or twice within twenty minutes of your performance. There are many formulas for calculating your maximum heart rate. Although not the most precise, one of the most common formulas is taking the number 220 minus your age. So if you are 40 years old, your would want to do an activity that briefly gets your heart rate up to 108-126 beats per minute (60-70% of (220-40)).

If this is new information for you, do not get caught up in the numbers. The idea is to quickly spike your physical system in a way that gets you ready to go without depleting energy. Run up and down a flight of stairs, take a brisk walk around the block, jump rope, or do some jumping jacks. With this type of light, brisk exercise, your body will quickly recover. Rather than physically draining your body, it will wake you up and help maintain energy during your performance. Of course you need to take into consideration your physical health. If you are out of shape or have a physical condition in which a spike in blood pressure or heart rate would present a danger, seek the advise of your healthcare provider in formulating safe ways to get your body warmed up for a performance.

6. Emotional Priming

Every top performer will attest to the importance and power of emotions. When you are emotionally strong, you are relaxed, focused, and brimming with confidence. You are on solid footing and ready to make things happen. You welcome any challenges that come before you.

As you prime yourself emotionally, you become more open to new ideas and information. You can more readily see another person's perspective. You become less focused on yourself and more interested in what others need and how you can help. With positive emotional priming, you move from selling to problem solving as your focus becomes all about identifying and meeting your client's needs.

Find the phrases that work for you to get your emotions in line with the task at hand. Here are some examples of statements used by my sales clients as part of their emotional priming:

> I love helping my clients!
> I am totally prepared and ready to do my best!
> I am internally strong and look confident!
> The greater the challenge, the more I love it!
> I love the process of selling as much as closing!
> Great product, trusted advisor!
> I'm a problem solver!
> Hammer away!
> Bring it on!
> Let's get after it!

What phrase, either borrowed from above or created anew works best for you? Emotion is a powerful driver. Use it. You will be successful in sales when you generate positive emotions and use these as the basis of forming an emotional connection with your clients. Also use emotional priming to establish a genuine emotional connection with your product. Top sales professionals know that selling is not about the product. It is the emotion surrounding the product and the relationship with the seller. This is what loyal clients buy: a recommendation that a product will improve their life from someone whom they emotionally connect with and trust.

7. Focal Point

You could quickly compile a list of possible distractions in your selling environment. These distractions can come from any direction at any time. What are those things that surround you and tend to pull you away from your task? Anything that pulls you out of your practiced strategy, even if it is a good thing, can be viewed as a distraction. Some distractions might be quite subtle, such as stopping a sales presentation to answer questions or follow other tangents. Once you have completed the question and answer series, you can use a focal point to quickly get back on track.

A focal point is a designated item in your performance arena used to bring you back to your strategy at hand. Before you perform, select an easily viewed

150

item to serve as a focal point. Your focal point ideally should be stationary. Depending on your performance arena, however, you might need to get creative and determine a focal point that will move with you. I have seen runners put a mark on their hand and rowers put a dot on the back of the teammate in front of them. The key is to make sure you will retain site of your focal point. A softball player who had just started to use this tool once told me about how she had forgotten this requirement. She chose a cloud as her focal point. When she found herself drifting away from her strategy and went looking for her focal point . . . it also had drifted off.

If you are in a conference room, you might choose a banner, a piece of art, or a clock on the wall. As you travel or perform in different locations, try to use the same type of focal point. Any time you get distracted, consciously look at your focal point. Train your mind to equate looking at that object with thinking, "OK, back to my strategy. Boom! I am back on task."

8. Performance Rehearsal

A performance rehearsal is the most comprehensive type of priming. This is where you fully engage your mind, body and emotions in preparation for your performance. This component is an important aspect of a pre-event routine. When done correctly, this piece is essential to putting you into "the zone" and a position of optimal performance.

Have you watched an elite athlete get ready for a competitive event? Perhaps you have watched an Olympic skier stand at the top of the jump waiting for his turn. He closes his eyes and makes small movements with his body as he sees performing the perfect jump. This athlete is rehearsing his performance in his mind, seeing the physical movements and feeling the emotions that accompanying a successful performance. He makes small turns with his shoulders as he sees himself perform the turns in his mind. He jerks his head back slightly as he sees himself lift into the air. He feels the air cold against his skin and the excitement of nailing the jump.

You would benefit from preparing in a similar way before making a big sales proposal. Shortly before your performance, take the time to perform in your mind. See yourself make the perfect sales proposal. Move your body in little movements. Your hand moves forward as you clearly see in your mind how you will approach your prospective client and introduce yourself. Feel the energy and excitement that accompanies a successful presentation. You are priming and activating your whole mind, body and emotions in preparation for your performance. This is an extremely effective way to prepare you to perform at your optimal level.

9. Engagement Cue

Up to this point of your routine, your mind, body and emotions are fully primed. This is necessary for peak performance, but not sufficient. An engagement cue is the last component in any practice or pre-event routine. It immediately precedes the performance and says, "Go!" This piece stands alone as a necessary component to peak performance. I have seen elite performers do everything right in preparing for a performance, but when it was time to perform, they forgot to tell themselves to turn it on. This inevitably leads to a less than stellar performance.

Put something in your performance arena that you physically cross before you perform. The idea is to link a thought (NOW!) with an action (GO!) to tell your mind, body and emotions that it is time to perform. You probably want to start with a tangible engagement cue. During my years of graduate school, my engagement cue was the doorframe on the building where my program was housed. Each time I walked into this door, whether for the first each morning or returning from lunch or an outdoor break, I engaged my mind. "Now! It's time to perform. Turn it on."

You want your cue to be portable. If you travel a lot, this will require you to pick an engagement cue that you can take with you or create a cue in your mind. Part of my company's logo is a red line. That line symbolizes the choice we make daily to perform at our highest level and help our clients do the same. It also serves as my personal engagement cue. Prior to a presentation or meeting, as I walk in the door or up to the podium, I imagine a red line on the floor. As I cross the line, I turn on my full engagement.

Depending on the circumstances, you might establish multiple engagement cues within a single performance arena. I have seen baseball teams use the last step of the dugout, while the pitcher would draw an additional line by the side of the mound. The pitcher would cross that line each inning and when he needed to re-engage during the game. You might have an engagement cue at the outside door of your office building and another one inside at the door to your office or the conference room. Train your mind to equate this engagement cue with flipping the ON switch.

10. Strategy Review

A strategy review is a post-event routine component. When you proactively build performance strategies, you can measure each performance by how well you executed your strategy. This process requires critical thinking. Make a detailed personal examination of your strategy execution. Talk to a trusted co-worker, manager or mentor about their observations.

What did your performance look like? Did you forget to properly prime your body, emotions or mind? Were you primed but forgot to properly engage?

Did you get so caught up in the dynamics of making introductions that you forgot to use your beginning strategy, but you got back to your strategy after the introductions? Did you get flustered and sidetracked with questions and forget to use your focal point to help get back on track? Do any of your strategies need to be tweaked? What are you going to do next time? This type of information provides a valuable starting point for making necessary corrections and improving future performance.

Your strategy review highlights the power of a prospective approach to performance. With a retrospective approach, you might lose a sale because you made a poor first impression. You were nervous because you were thinking about the desired outcome ("I *need* to make this sale"). Given your focus on the outcomes, you did not have a specific strategy in place. By the time the potential client walked out the door, you had decided that you did a lousy job overall and were experiencing a general sense of failure. As you beat yourself up, these self destructive and nonproductive feelings snowball. From this hazy cloud of emotion, you decide to scrap everything you just tried. It didn't work after all.

A prospective approach, on the other hand, would empower you to review your strategy execution and observe, "I did not follow my strategy for the start of my presentation. I need to give this area more attention." With clarity, you can see your mistake and see that you are nowhere near a failure. You just have a thing or two to work on. Think of how much better you will feel and how much more productive you will be when you can identify with precision areas of necessary improvement. A strategy review helps you identify the pieces of your strategy or performance that need attention so you can quickly put a plan in place to improve and get ready for your next sales performance.

Types of Routines

You can use some or all of the above components to create a preparation or practice routine to use everyday to help maximize your daily performance. Think about the types of activities you frequently encounter during your day or week. These routines might address administrative, sales, service and marketing activities. Establishing routines for sleep, nutrition, exercise and travel can quickly create higher levels of energy. Establishing personal routines for home, family and spirituality will facilitate a more integrated and fulfilling life.

In addition to multiple daily preparation routines, create separate pre-event routines to use before a particular performance. You might build a pre-event routine for giving a presentation, attending a meeting, making a sales proposal or even utilizing a block of time for calling, research, writing or putting together a proposal.

The final type of performance routine, the post-event routine, is powerful when performing multiple events. It is rare for salespeople not to have multiple sales calls, presentations, appointments and other activities within a single day. Learn how to briefly take time after each activity to review your strategy execution, make necessary adjustments, discharge any negative emotions and refuel your energy level.

The reality is that you already incorporate routines or some sort of ritualistic behavior in your work (and personal) life, even if you don't call it a routine. If you cannot identify any of your routines, ask those closest to you what you consistently do every morning upon arriving at work or every time you prepare for an appointment. Take some time to identify these elements and the information provided in this chapter to revise and add additional components to strengthen your routines.

As part of this process, become aware of any bad habits or maladaptive routines you have established along the way. At the top of the list are the misuse of drugs, alcohol and food as relaxation or coping techniques. A close companion is the use of stimulants, including caffeine and adrenaline, to compensate for a lack of high quality sleep. More subtle examples abound, from skipping breakfast to overuse of the Internet. Scour your daily activities for any routine actions that undermine your performance. Changing maladaptive routines that do not appropriately prepare your mind, body and emotions for performing at a high level can provide a quantum leap forward in your performance.

If you manage people, establish team routines with your staff. Help individuals on your team establish positive routines that support these staff routines. Once your staff has solid strategies in place and established routines to protect strategy execution, it is your role as manager to protect these routines. When it's time to perform, make sure you keep others and yourself out of the way so your sales professionals can perform their routines. You will generate a higher level of consistent team performance than you have ever experienced.

Summary

Now you have a better understanding of how strategies and routines work together to optimally engage your mind, body and emotions to perform the task at hand. Strategies provide the process to produce the desired outcome. Routines keep you focused on your strategies and protect you from influences and distractions. Make sure that your individual strategies and performance routines are built in a way that is consistent with your values. This will increase your sales performance while resulting in a deep level of daily fulfillment.

Chapter Thirteen

Fueling Your Success – Managing Time and Energy

You can't give away what you don't have. This is one of those universal truths in life that when you come to truly appreciate it, you will begin to notice its many applications in different areas of your life and the powerful impact that it can have. Even though it's a concept that goes well beyond the improvement of your time management skills, you will discover that as you learn to more efficiently use your time, you begin to structure your day in a way that creates more for your life. Once you can efficiently use your time to create more energy, you will then be in a position to do more, feel more, give more and become more.

In my consulting practice, I find that when clients constantly feel that they have "no time" to do the things they want in life, the issue is more about energy management than time management. They jam so much into their day and simply wear themselves out trying to get it all done. They ignore their need to stop and refuel along the way. Would you try to drive your car without filling it with gas or regularly changing the oil? Of course not! You would get stranded, probably at the least opportune time, putting yourself in a position of being unable to go where you are trying to go. Just like your automobile, your mind, body, emotions and spirit also need refueling on a regular basis. When you don't do this, no matter how much you want to do something, you'll find yourself stranded, unable to achieve the task.

You now have an idea of what can go wrong, but now take a moment to really think through what you could gain from learning how to effectively manage your energy. Even if you are performing toward the top of your field, there is still a gap between where you currently operate and your optimal level of energy creation. This gap is brimming with opportunities and as you close this gap, you become closer to living your full potential.

Earlier in the book, we talked about the importance of achieving daily goals in making you the best sales professional and person you can be. You learned that it is important to schedule tasks on the day in which they need to be completed. Daily goals are the things you need to get done during the day or else they will keep you up at night. Of course, we don't want that to happen. And yet, because these are activities that you have identified to help you become the person you want to become and achieve what you want to achieve, it should be unsettling not to complete them. You need to get them done.

Time is a precious and consumable resource. As every minute of your life passes, there is no way to recover it or know how much time you have remaining which makes it so important to use your time wisely. Doing so increases productivity, which increases your financial gain. It also increases efficiency, which frees up additional time to spend with the people you love and on the activities you enjoy. For all of these reasons, it is worth learning how to best manage your time in order to achieve your daily goals.

We all have had experiences of hyper-productivity that highlight the power of thinking through our priorities, identifying what we really want to accomplish to support those priorities, and progressively completing those tasks. What times of hyper-productivity stand out in your mind? Perhaps it was in preparation for meeting a tight deadline? Or perhaps the last full day in the office before a vacation or extended leave?

What made you so effective in those instances? Chances are that you took the time to sit down and write out a list of what you wanted to accomplish that day. Think about how productive you would be if you harnessed that type of focus and energy every day.

Have you ever crossed paths with one of those rare individuals who seems to create more time and get more done than humanly possible? These people have mastered the art of energy creation. Optimizing energy creation can take you from poor to good, from good to great, from great to stellar, and from stellar to off the charts! Let's take a look at some of the keys to managing time and energy that can place you in that category of rare individuals with seemingly endless amounts of time and energy.

Honor Yourself

When people think of honoring, or taking care of, themselves, they generally think of things like diet and sleep. These are essential functions, as your body will not operate efficiently without being properly fueled. This includes a need for adequate hydration. Often times when you think you are hungry, you really are thirsty. Sufficient water intake stands alone as a necessary biological need. Every system in your body depends on regular consumption of this essential nutrient.

Similarly, sleep (especially the lack of it) is a huge issue for sales professionals. If sleep quantity or quality is a problem for you, move away from the position of being a victim of your circumstances and take control of the situation. Begin with taking common sense actions like reducing or eliminating caffeine. Ensure that your sleep environment is comfortable, dark and conducive to a good night's sleep. Create a pre-sleep routine to effectively wind down each night. If you are not getting enough done during the day and it's keeping you awake at night, begin using the system discussed below to ensure you complete your daily goals. If you still wake up with things on your

156

mind, keep a notepad by your bed and dump any thoughts onto that. Those items will be there for you in the morning and you can turn back to the task at hand – refueling your body with essential sleep. If you think your sleep disruption problem is physically based, seek assistance from your health care professional.

New research continues to mount on the negative effects of insufficient sleep, including evidence that suggests sleep deprivation can suppress your immune system, negatively affect memory and speed the aging process. It should be obvious by now that a lack of sleep will also make you less effective as a sales person. With insufficient sleep, your performance will continue to slowly take a nosedive as your body simply adapts to a lower and lower level of performance. Do what you need to do to meet and protect your need for sufficient high-quality sleep. Think about how much more you will get done when you wake up feeling rested, refreshed, alert, and ready to take on the day!

Not only is it a way of honoring yourself, but it also just makes sense that becoming the best version of yourself requires that your basic biological needs are met. So much more could be said in the areas of meeting these basic biological needs for sleep and nutrition. Fortunately, as there is solid advice available in these areas, including resources accessible by Internet, there is no excuse not to educate yourself. The issue this chapter will give more attention to is an area that is commonly overlooked or misunderstood: the concept of using stress to make yourself stronger, create more energy and achieve more of your potential.

Using Stress to Grow

Many people try to avoid stress. They avoid challenging situations in an attempt to eliminate stress from their life. They try to dull the effects of stress with the use of drugs, alcohol, pain medication or other numbing techniques. But eliminating stress is not what works in the real world. The world demands that in order to keep up, you need to grow in your tolerance for stress. As you progress through life, stress increases. This is a good thing. You want it to increase because as the challenges get bigger, so do the opportunities for growth.

Think about the current demands in your life compared to five years ago and five years before that. Looking back at those good old college days that preceded "the real world," it seems that life was such a breeze. But at the time you transitioned from high school to college, all of that extra homework certainly did not feel all that breezy. Over the course of your college years, you grew in your ability to handle the greater workload. This was necessary to earn your degree and, most likely, you also found it rewarding. However, many people go about their lives pulling away from as much stress as possible. While this might bring an initial sense of relief, it will quickly undermine your success in sales and overall performance. Reducing your exposure to stress will hinder your performance and lower your tolerance for challenge and growth. In short, you will get less done, be less healthy, make fewer sales, earn less money and be less satisfied with your life.

There are numerous daily activities that provide stress and the opportunity for growth when used correctly, because you can get too much of a good thing. Overdoing these activities can quickly cause them to become a negative influence. What are the areas in your life that involve "too much" or "over" behaving? Perhaps it is overeating, overlifting, oversleeping, overdrinking, overworking, overwatching T.V., oversurfing the net, overthinking or overreacting. For example, eating is necessary to fuel your body and provides energy to carry out life's tasks. Overeating will hinder you from performing those same tasks. Lifting weights improves your health and makes you stronger while overlifting weakens you and sets you up for injury. If you undertake an activity and do too much of it without sufficient rest, your performance will decrease.

Doing any activity without pairing it with sufficient rest can turn stress into what is known as distress. Distress requires building in a recovery period in which you simply get your body back to baseline. You can not move forward and take your performance to a higher level until you eliminate, or at least actively manage, distress. If you are in a condition of distress, do not try to plow through it with sheer grit. Stop. Figure out what you need to do to recover and put a plan in place. Focus on healing and getting yourself back to a neutral position and from there you can start to once again build to a higher level.

When you welcome stress into your life and regularly recoup your energy with appropriate rest, guess what happens? Factors and influences that used to be very difficult become challenging. You continue to grow. Then it's time to take on even more challenging tasks and welcome even more opportunities for growth. This will lead to a successful career in sales and make life a whole lot more fun along the way.

At what level do you welcome stress into your life? I want you to become a stress seeker! First, look at your mental workout. Is your work challenging? If you spend some time each day thinking, strategizing and problem solving, then good. On the other hand, if you are so used to the mental demands of your job that you simply go through the motions, then you need additional mental stress. (You also might need a new job!) Pick any activity that you enjoy to exercise your mind – crossword or sudoku puzzles, learning a foreign language, reading books or listening to DVDs. Of course, when keeping in mind your goals, some types of mental stress are more productive than others. For example, you could use your mind to brainstorm ways to improve your community as easily as you could use it to write a letter to the editor complaining about everything that is wrong in your community. Or you could spend mental energy building an

Internet business that would provide future security as easily as you could read the latest nonfiction bestseller. The choice of activities is going to be driven by your priorities and personal direction. The important thing is that you need to somehow stimulate your mind every day.

Similarly, daily exercise is essential to health and growth. You need to exercise your body on a daily basis to avoid becoming physically stagnate. Research continues to grow about the numerous short-term and long-term health benefits of regular physical exercise. If this type of stress currently is not a part of your day, you need to schedule it in and just do it.

Building In Rest

Rest is any activity, in and of itself, which is pleasurable and restorative. The rest has to follow the appropriate duration and form of the stress. This might mean lying down and taking a nap after running an all day sales conference. After a four-hour sales presentation, it might suffice to refuel with a good meal and spend time talking and laughing with friends. An hour at the office answering incoming calls or meeting with a client would require less rest. In this case, perhaps enjoy a cup of tea or do some stretching in your office.

Keep in mind that what is restful to one person might not be restful to you. Generate a list of activities that refuel and energize you. Some of these activities will include active rest, such as going for a walk, playing tennis or gardening. Others will include passive rest, which could mean time spent reading, playing a musical instrument or watching a movie. In order to perform at your optimal level, you must use these activities each and every day as a way to recoup the energy you expend along the way.

The most common question I hear from corporate clients after they have been introduced to the concept of stress-rest cycles is this: "Can I get my stress in during the week and then build in my rest cycle over the weekend?" The answer is NO! The key to growth is building both stress and rest into each day. You will not experience growth if you deplete yourself throughout the workweek, even if you try to load your weekend with fun and rest. Your performance level will decline over time.

There are a couple unique types of rest that frequently are overlooked but merit special care and attention: social time and spiritual time.

Social Time

The need for social time may be less obvious than activities like exercise, eating healthy, and getting your sleep, but your need for human interaction is equally important. Schedule social time in on a daily basis. Human beings are social animals and when you interact with others in a positive way it can provide instant rejuvenation.

Research shows that people with social support are healthier. They recover faster. They live longer. This may be in part because we use social time for so many things. It is a time for celebration; it allows you to share the fruits of your hard work with those you love. It is a time for support; you can debrief with others, process your disappointments and get re-energized to keep fighting the good fight. It is a time for humor; laughter unleashes an amazing restorative process as it changes the chemistry in your body.

Every day, build in time to personally interact closely with others. Spending time in person is best, but talking by telephone, emailing or texting also can help rejuvenate. Have lunch with a co-worker, walk with a friend or call someone to tell her that you are thinking of her. Sales people are fortunate because so much of their day typically involves interacting with others. When these interactions are positive, they can help refuel you. Just be aware that if a social interaction becomes negative, it serves as a form of stress and you need to build in additional rest to recover from it. When you take the time to include connection into each day, your life becomes richer and more productive.

Spiritual Time

Spiritual time is a special form of rest. It is time for you to be by yourself and refuel in a way that works for you. You do not share this time with your co-workers, best friend, spouse or kids. This is your time. You can fill it with centering activities, such as prayer, meditation, or yoga. You can engage in self-development activities, such as reading, listening to CDs, watching DVDs, or journaling. You can take time for a hobby that connects you to a larger creative force, such as painting, playing an instrument, or writing. One executive I know spent his spiritual time fly tying. Over time, he created hundreds of intricate fly fishing hooks, not to use but to center himself in the process and give his mind and body a rejuvenating rest.

Begin with a minimum of 15 minutes every day and work up to a half-hour. Be selfish with this important rest cycle. You will be tempted to disregard this, thinking that you are too busy. It is the first thing I see people drift away from when their life gets overly scheduled. I know from experience how challenging it is to carve out these precious minutes of "me time" within each day. Yet the rejuvenation produced will increase your energy and your payback will be much greater than the time you gave to the activity. Figure out which part of your day works best for you. It might be first thing in the morning, the last thing at night, during your lunch break or right after work. By making yourself a priority in this way, you will create more energy to give to projects that you want to complete and to your loved ones.

160

Daily Goal System

Once you have started taking care of the things you need to do on a daily basis to honor yourself and create more energy, it is helpful to put into place a strategy to make the best use of your time. You have built a foundation of high energy. Following are four steps to best channel that energy in order to optimize your potential and produce results.

Step 1: Honor Today

With every turn of your daily calendar, make it a practice of honoring the passage of time. Center yourself on the precious gift of another day of life and the opportunities that the day holds. You are acknowledging another day peeling off of the calendar, forever now beyond your reach. When we are not conscious of the passage of time, which so easily happens as we get caught up in the details of our life, the minutes and hours tick off the clock, one day after another. Another day slips through our fingers. How many times have you begun writing out a check or filling out a document only to need to stop and think, "What day is it?"

Do not let this day get away from you. Don't allow yourself to be consumed with reacting to other people's priorities or the minor urgencies that seem to surface on any given day. Take time on a daily basis to recommit to your most important priorities. Break down the steps and goals needed to meet these priorities. Honor the day you have been given by making a commitment that the passage of time within the next twenty-four hours will be accompanied by real and measurable growth toward realizing your goals and potential.

Step 2: Identify and Declare Your Intent

Begin your daily planning by looking ahead over the next month or so and identifying your number one short-term goal. What project do you most want to complete? What sales level do you want to achieve? In what part of your life do you need a wake-up call or a reminder about where you want to go? What values do you want to further? What relationship do you want to nurture? What bad habit do you want to replace with a good habit?

Establishing your value-based direction addressed earlier in the book will lead the way in this assessment. Take that goal and make it into a broader intention statement by merging it with that larger desire that is burning within you. Your intention statement includes a reflection of why this goal is so important. For example, you choose to prioritize your short-term goal of selling ten percent more products this month. Your intention statement might read, "I am now selling 10% more products each month to better use my potential and build security for my family." If your goal is to start an Internet business from

161

home and a first necessary step is to set up a home office, your intention might be, "I am creating an organized and productive office space which will energize me and the development of my company."

Emotion is an important part of stating your intention. Give careful thought to both your broader intent and your wording. Take a moment to emotionally align with your statement. This intention is important to you for a reason. Nod your head and affirm your direction. "Yes, this is what I want and I am making it happen!" Feel energized by the challenge you are setting before you.

Step 3: Commit to Three Critical Daily Priorities

List the three most important actions you can take today to support the achievement of your intention. I call these criticals. Make these items intentional, conscious choices. As you write your three criticals, commit to achieving each of these things before the end of the day.

Write your criticals with a spirit of integrity. Isn't it important to you to be a person who can be trusted to do what you say you are going to do? Take pride in being a person who can be counted on. You are making this promise to the most important person in your life – yourself. You have an obligation to become the best you can be in this life. You also know, with a properly aligned personal direction, that as you become more and achieve more, you will give more to everyone else in your life.

Limit this list to three items because you do not want to over promise what you will get done each day. These items represent a minimum level of what you will achieve on a given day. The process of writing these actions down and committing to them, with a spirit of integrity, will wake up your mind and convince your subconscious that you are serious about fulfilling your intention and achieving your goals.

Check your criticals off as completed. Celebrate the accomplishment of each one! Completing these priorities represent solid steps toward achieving larger goals. When you celebrate crossing off these items and feel that feeling of accomplishment, good things happen in your brain's reward center. Generating these feelings of success on a daily basis will provide motivation to keep you moving forward.

Step 4: Commit to Additional Daily Actions

In addition to your three criticals, list all other items that you want to achieve today. These items, which I call dailys, typically include items like meetings, correspondence, phone calls, research and planning items, relationship maintenance activities and errands. Similar to your criticals, you are committing to complete these items before your head hits the pillow at night. These things are important and you are going to give full efforts toward completing them within the day. You do not want to complete these activities, however, at the cost of crowding out your critical priorities. Your criticals are the actions you have identified as being most essential to achieving what you truly want to achieve in life. Use your dailys to complement this forward movement. Depending on your schedule for the day, your dailys might include a few additional smaller steps to help support your larger daily intention. Remember to check off each item as you complete it. Great job! Now on to the next!

Using a line to separate your critical priorities from your other daily goals can result in an empowering change in how you look at things. This is because it is the nature of many items that end up on a typical "to do" list to crowd out our true priorities. This process can help you value your time more and also help you see how you may be using the busy-work of life as an excuse for why you are not being more productive. Say, for example, that you identify prospecting activities as one of your critical priorities. After doing this activity on a more regular basis, it becomes clear that just one hour of prospecting calls consistently turns into three appointments and one sale. For years, you also have taken time each week to mow your lawn. This type of house maintenance activity is a typical "to-do" item. However, when you see that the sale generated from one hour of prospecting puts $500 in your pocket and your child or the neighbor's child will mow your lawn for $10, delegating items that use to appear on your "to do" list starts to make much more sense.

In order to maximize the power of this four-step process, you need to repeat it daily. Establish a routine for reviewing your goals, forming your intent, identifying three critical actions and generating your list of daily actions. Do this in a way that works best for you. Get up a little earlier than usual to make it happen. Pair it with your morning cup of coffee. Think through your intentions and daily goals as you exercise or while showering and then take the time to WRITE them down. The power is in writing them down, keeping this reminder with you throughout the day, and holding yourself to a high standard of personal integrity to do what you have said you will do.

This process in action might look like this:

Honor today: (Write out today's full date and acknowledge its personal significance.)

Identify and declare intent: Establish professional web presence as sales advisor to increase credibility and enhance the growth of my sales business.

Commit to Criticals:
1) Complete minimum of 20 prospecting calls.
2) Research web designers and schedule interviews with top 2-3 candidates.
3) Draft professional bio for website.

Commit to Dailys:
Brainstorm and create list of 10 possible domain names, research successful sales advisor websites, outline website structure, return and make phone calls, take son to lunch, surprise wife with flowers, check email a.m. and p.m. and respond, schedule doctor's appointment

Can you see how this process would complement your current time management system? It both helps you make decisions about how to spend your time and keeps your goal setting connected to your core values and vision. This will increase your productivity while ensuring that all of your goals are headed in the same direction. Make conscious decisions daily about prioritization rather than changing your focus haphazardly as you respond to deadlines and shifting demands. Although some goals you focus on will carry urgency, each of them should carry importance and relevance to your life plan. Each goal you set must fit into the big picture you have for your life. If it does not, then you will not be sufficiently motivated to make it happen.

Do not make this process more complex than it needs to be. I used to plan out my day on a separate piece of paper in my planner. Then a colleague of mine (thanks, Dr. Phil Humbert) showed me how handy those little 3x5 index cards are and I now use those by the stack for all types of things. I take fifteen minutes or so every morning and sit down with my planner and an index card. I reflect and then write my long-term intention on one side of the card. I flip the card over and write my three critical daily actions on top, separated by a line from the list of additional daily actions. I then carry my card with me during the day to check off items (that feels good!), add items or write notes. Make this process your own as you unleash its power to create amazing levels of daily motivation and performance

When you harness the power of managing your energy and managing your time, you will increase your productivity. In sales, productivity directly relates to profitability. The amount of time spent in planning produces a huge return on investment. When you do not know exactly what you want to accomplish during your day, you are more subject to outside influences and distractions. Other people who have given thought to what they want to achieve will impose upon you with their requests to have you meet their objectives. Worse, those who have given no thought to planning their day will impose on you as they stop to visit about this or that. These types of distractions will decrease your effectiveness. Using the tools in this chapter on a daily basis can lead to a higher level of sales, more money and greater job satisfaction.

Should you ever take a break from this system? It might be tempting to think on those "really busy" days that you can run through this process in your head. Yet if you are feeling so rushed that you cannot set aside a few minutes to renew your direction and set your daily priorities, are you really likely to get the most important things crossed off your list that day?

How about when on vacation or when traveling? I think that these situations provide you all the more reason to honor the day and think through what you want to do while in a new or different place. If you are with your family or friends, what activities will refuel your relationships with them? How can you create memories that you will talk about for years to come? Only you know these answers. Do you want to bungee jump in New Zealand, paraglide in Hawaii, or collect seashells with your children along the coast of Florida?

Planning today while keeping your big picture in mind will make you happier and healthier. It also will make you more productive, putting you in a position to reap more monetary rewards. This increased income can be spent to enrich other areas of your life, allowing you to save and spend in ways that promote your values – whether that means making more money, spending time with family and friends, volunteering in your community or traveling the world.

Summary

Make sure that you are including within each day all of the components necessary for optimal performance. Build in sufficient mental and physical stress with appropriate rest. Begin by meeting your biological need for sleep. When formulating rest cycles, make a conscious choice to include social time and spiritual time as forms of rest. Experiment with the type of activity and amount of time spent on it. Create a system that works for you and make it part of a prospective approach to high sales performance.

Successful sales professionals create and use systems for their success. They understand the importance of consistently taking meaningful action on a daily basis. They appreciate that small or simple actions can make a big difference over time. Use the advice in this book to improve all aspects of your life – physical, mental, emotional and spiritual. Use the energy you create by building in stress and appropriate rest cycles coupled with the time you free up by building a blueprint for each day to take your sales performance to a higher and higher level.

Chapter Fourteen

Rituals of Customer Acquisition

To be successful in sales, you must be actively seeking new customer opportunities. Your current employer has a significant investment in you and you have a significant investment in yourself. Activity management speaks to everything that precedes the actual sales meeting with the customer. There are certain behaviors, attitudes and processes that successful sales professionals demonstrate that get them the activity necessary to become successful in sales.

Prospecting

If you speak with corporate sales trainers and very successful sales experts, one thing will be unanimous among the top professionals. Sales appointments don't lead to sales; prospects do.

Successful sales experts equate that 45% of their overall sales effort is prospecting and an additional 20% of their sales effort is spent making presentations. This means that successful sales experts spend 65% of their time developing opportunities and identifying if there is a fit.

One of the biggest challenges for many sales people is a low level of sales activity. In other words, sales people will express their biggest challenge is not having enough customers to visit. The effect of not seeing enough people leads to consistently missing quota targets, making less commission one month while missing the next and experiencing the ups and downs as well as the highs and lows that play emotionally on every sales rep's mind throughout the selling month.

All of this goes away with a disciplined approach towards prospecting. If you don't prospect, you don't have anyone to meet with. It's that simple.

Yet arguably, prospecting reluctance seems to be an Achilles heel for many sales professionals. Prospecting can be fun, exciting and simple. You just need to make it a priority within your sales day. Top sales experts book time off each day to prospect. This demonstrates that the most important appointment each day is the one you make with yourself, to prospect.

Sales reps often do not find time to prospect, citing that the day has other priorities. Here's the simple answer: you must find personal time to locate prospects. Prospecting is as important to a sales rep as gas is to a car. Failure to regularly replenish your fuel means that you will eventually run out of gas.

Running out of gas equates to a loss of momentum – literally to a stand still. Selling is all about momentum.

You should view prospecting positively. It should be fun and strategic and have a purpose. Most sales people are creative and that should be exactly how you approach prospecting. By being creative in your approach, you will open doors and opportunities that other sales professionals wouldn't explore. After all, all you are doing is your job.

But how, where and how often should you be prospecting?

Let's begin with how often should you be prospecting? The answer is always. In fact, when you think about it, everyone that you meet could be a possible prospect or knows someone that could be a prospect. This stands true when you realize that on average, every person that you know will know an additional 250 people. We know this because that is the average attendance at a funeral. Never dismiss any opportunity, no matter how trivial it may seem on the surface, to let people know what you do.

Prospecting for new account opportunities can be found in many ways. Let's look at a few of them.

Associations

Joining an association is a great idea and an excellent way to prospect for new opportunities. You must get involved however and not sit by the wayside as an audience member. You should be presenting to other members of the association on a regular basis.

Normally, you wouldn't join an association where your peers attend. For instance, if you were selling life insurance, you wouldn't join an association where other life insurance agents attend. Pick a completely different association where you can be perceived as a resource and have no immediate competition. Develop a unique offer specific to the association that caters to the top three areas of concern that members are experiencing.

Because you will be presenting at these events, it would be advisable to be comfortable delivering a presentation in front of large groups of people. If necessary, you can always improve your skills by taking a public speaking course. The benefit of delivering a speech is that after you are done, people will already pre qualify themselves as a customer and approach you and want to meet with you. Remember that if you are going to join an association, you have to be prepared to invest the time required to be effective.

Trade Shows

Industry trade shows are a great area to develop leads. You can approach prospecting at trade shows from two separate angles - as a vendor and as an attendee.

Vendor

As a vendor, your company will have made a significant financial investment for you and others to represent your company and service. Leads generated from the show are usually divided among the booth representatives. In some instances, you get to keep the prospect opportunities with those you meet at the show.

Working a trade show isn't easy if you don't have the right mindset. It is tiring work and typically a long day. Many times, there is no place to sit, no under pad below the carpeting and the internal temperatures can vary from too hot to too cold.

The upside is that trade shows are specific in interest. Attendees are highly qualified prospects. Figuratively speaking, you can cover a lot of ground without actually going far. It also allows you the opportunity to have others approach you versus cold calling and other prospecting methods.

Attendee

This is a very successful and under utilized prospecting opportunity. As a visitor, you have the ability to visit hundreds of prospects in a short period of time. As an attendee, you will be meeting people in the booths who are either decision makers or can direct you to the names and numbers of key contacts that otherwise you may spend more time and effort trying to reach. You can also unlock opportunities that otherwise you may have passed up, simply because you didn't know the company existed or what the company did. In addition, you can get to attend seminars and gain industry information that you otherwise may have missed. It also serves as a great way to visit existing customers who may be vendors at the show.

Being prepared and staying focused on your purpose for being there is the key to prospecting successfully at any trade show. Have a specific goal in mind. You may set a goal indicating exactly how many business cards you get. You may wish to set a goal of getting the internal contacts within a certain division. The key is to have a target to achieve and not to be restricted to a time line. You have to be flexible, so book in activity throughout the day that allows you to accomplish this. Remember, leave when you have met your desired goal and not before.

Visit your local convention center's website regularly. There will be a calendar of events that outline details of the upcoming trade shows. You can also access additional links to other official websites sponsoring these events.

Direct Mail

Direct mail can be an effective prospecting tool. Many view this form of prospecting financially risky because of the high cost associated with print and postage. It is advisable to consider targeting smaller groups at the beginning of launching a larger campaign to test the overall success and response rates.

Here are a few ways to maximize your overall success using direct mail. First, you must have a great sales copy. You are writing a commercial in print, which must be effective. In the end, you must compel your customer to take action. This may be them calling you or them accepting your call. In any event, writing a great sales copy will determine success or failure.

Test your market audience first and measure your response rate. Sending out 1000 pieces of mail to prospective customers and expecting to call all of them back in two weeks will not be reasonable. Smaller test runs at the beginning will help you gauge what the optimum distribution frequency and response rates will be.

You must not get discouraged if customers are not getting your literature. There are several hands that touch your direct mail piece before your customer does. The post office, internal mail department and the executive assistant can all become obstacles in the arrival of your information getting into the right hands.

If you are getting better than a 2% success rate on your direct mail, you are doing well.

Networking

Networking with potential prospects can be in many forms. We have all found ourselves in a situation where we are at a function or get together where great prospects are in attendance. For some, this can be a nerve-racking experience. For others, it's not an issue to be in an environment where they do not know anyone.

Once again, when at an event where the goal is to prospect for opportunities, you must be prepared and have a goal. A little research ahead of time goes a long way. With research you will develop a strategy. You may identify one or two key candidates who are top priority of the evening. Being committed to your goal ensures that you will meet with those people and exceed your objectives.

Setting up a network club is also a great idea. This is where you and other sales people from various industries get together and share leads. These meetings are generally organized and scheduled. Quite often these sessions can be simple and could be set up with breakfast meetings. In the larger network clubs, there are organized dinners and guest speakers in attendance. In either event, large or small, these meetings are a great way to exchange leads, be introduced to new prospects and have a great support network in sales as well.

Sales experts work on developing networking skills. There are many areas of personal development that will help you become an expert and fearless. Some typical areas to develop include:

- Public Speaking
- Social Etiquette
- Body Language
- Story Telling

Telemarketing

In sales, one of the most cost effective and efficient ways to prospect is over the telephone. It comes with a price however. It can be one of the most nerve-racking experiences that a sales person can encounter.

Many sales people get a mental block in their head with respect to cold calling over the phone. Many equate this activity as "bothering" someone the same way that many of us feel when we are being disturbed at home, usually around six while having dinner. That is bothersome – agreed.

However, when you are conducting business, during business hours, with other business owners, it is expected that solicitation of services takes place. After all, you believe that your product, service or offer is the best – right? You are paid by your company to reach out to people and share the good news – right? And finally, your customer has a responsibility to their employer or business to seek out ways to be more efficient, productive, profitable, secure, safe and so on – right?

Well then there is a match. What you are doing is perfectly acceptable and expected by customers. So why the mental block with respect to telemarketing?

It's rather simple. First, it begins with the mindset of the sales person as they approach the call. Second it begins by the sales person accepting that telemarketing is a skill. To book an appointment with someone that you have never met with before, who you believe is a strong prospect, is a skill. Once mastered, it will be invaluable.

Here are a few simple rules for telemarketing new prospects:

- Smile – it makes a BIG difference
- Mindset – you are here to help
- Do a little every day (1 hour per day)
- Be prepared and organized before you begin
- Don't stop – momentum is everything
- It's not personal – people can be rude

171

Here is a helpful hint that often gets dismissed immediately by sales people. Write out a short script. I know, you probably just thought "a script, no that's not me". Here is a question. What was the last movie that you saw, that you really liked? What did you like about it? Did it capture you emotionally and were you captivated? Was there a script?

Sure, great movies begin and end with a script. Actors recite their part over and over until it is perfect and comes across in a natural manner. Telemarketing is a skill that can be effectively learned – quickly. Don't worry about your personality not coming through with the end result. It will! A great telemarketing course takes one day to complete. Those skills that you develop will go far beyond just telephone skills and well worth the investment of your personal time.

Personal Time Management

Getting an appointment with a customer takes a lot of effort on behalf of the sales professional. Be it a cold call or warm call, there is time associated with the effort. Likewise, when an appointment is booked, there is time and effort invested in the sales meeting by both you and your customer.

Both of you must commit to honor that time. In many cases, the duration of a sales call in the business to a business sales call generally is booked for one hour. That being said, it is not uncommon to have some sales professionals book 30-minute meetings with their customers. This is dependent on your sales process and nature of your sale although I do however question this; how effective is a first appointment if it is only booked for 30 minutes?

Consider this. You ask your customer for a 60-minute meeting and they agree. You arrive on time and they meet you in the reception area on time. From this point of time, the stopwatch begins. It takes a minute or two to walk to the office. Another 4-7 minutes to exchange pleasantries and idle chit chat as you get to know the customer a little better. Then you begin the meeting. The meeting is going along well and with 15 minutes left, you begin to summarize your points of discussion. With 10 minutes to go, you review the next steps and take-away agenda items while discussing any last minute changes. Finally with 5 minutes left, you get off topic completely and wind down the call only to be escorted back to reception with two minutes to go.

Quickly, you realize that the 60-minute call only had 40-45 minutes of sales time. When you work these factors into an agreed 30-minute sales call, time becomes even more of the essence. Therefore, it becomes paramount that you are prepared with great questions so that you uncover maximum information in a minimum amount of time.

Time is the most important currency that we have in sales. Sales experts pay very close attention to how they manage their entire day. They do not work a 9-5 day. They manage their day efficiently and work smart. Effectively balancing your priorities and time will always remain the difference between the successful sales expert and the happy under achiever.

Territory Management

To be effective in selling, you have to manage whom you see and when you see them. Therefore, careful planning will allow you to maximize your time and effort as well as results.

Territory management requires planning on your part. You need to know what geographic areas you need to visit and the necessary time for travel. Sales experts take into consideration rush hour times, construction, flow of traffic and other variables that affect maximizing your time and effort.

Break up your territory into smaller groups. Some companies do not assign geographic regions and allow everyone to sell everywhere. In either case, you must plan out where you are calling – strategically. Directories are available which allow you to sort names by company, vertical market, city, town, zip code, size or revenue. Use these tools to maximize efficiency and increase your "face time" with your customer.

Account Management

Demonstrate Distinct Value

Sales experts are always trying to demonstrate distinct value to the customer. They are always thinking about adding value, which is outside of the "Me Too" realm of selling. Sales experts realize that not everything revolves around their product/service and offering. Building rapport, trust and likeability goes far beyond "selling".

Imagine the value you demonstrate if you were to inform your customer of up to date information before they even heard about it. This could be related to anything of interest to your customer.

Informing your customer of any business related industry or company news specifically, will demonstrate that you are in the know and resourceful which further adds credibility to you, personally.

I recall the time that I congratulated a customer on a recent acquisition that their company had just announced. He wrote back immediately "thanks for letting me know. We hadn't heard anything officially yet over here." I sent him the link where the article was posted. He was able to share this information with his peers and team and ended up looking like a hero. Even his boss was not in the know yet. The company's marketing department was alerted to the premature news leak and immediately took action, all because of his tip.

Setting up simple yet effective strategies can make you distinct in what you offer. Quite often this is accomplished with little or no financial investment on your part. A simple email, voice mail or connected call is all that it takes to show the customer that you actually care enough and are resourceful as to what is happening.

Every response from a customer by returned phone call, email or voice mail further insulates the competition from penetrating "your" account even further.

Finding out what the customer's personal hobbies and interests are goes a long way. This is where you have a wonderful opportunity to "ground yourself" with your customer.

If your customer expresses a sincere interest in bowling, then find three other customers who like to bowl and host a bowling night. Likewise, if your customer likes to fish, find three other customers who have a passion for fishing and set up a small tournament. Quite often, these events become annual events that your busy customers eagerly look forward to.

Persuasive sellers also utilize existing customers strategically to assist in the development of new business opportunities and insulate against the competition.

Finally, sales experts are people and opportunity connectors. This means that they connect people into each others social and business circles thus unlocking countless other areas to explore and mine for business opportunities

30 Second Commercial

Imagine this. You get on an elevator with a potential executive that you want to meet. At the very least, they would be a great referral internally and would be able to open doors if you had them sponsor you within the account. The elevator door closes and you make eye contact. He says hello and you say hello. What are you going to say next?

Just for a moment consider this scenario. You are at a wedding where your cousin is getting married. Your extended family is there. You realize that your other cousin, whom you have not met in several years, is sitting four tables next to you. You know that he just purchased a 10 million dollar business. You know he is a prime candidate and user of your product and service. The issue is that this is not the time to discuss business; however you do want to exchange business cards and secure the next step. You know that once you do meet him, he will probably ask you, "...so what have you been up to – it's been a while hasn't it?" What would you say?

If you had a prepared and well-rehearsed 30-second commercial, you would be able to begin the conversation and at the very least, exchange business cards and hopefully secure the next step.

A scripted short commercial on yourself and what you can offer is necessary to have at any time. In sales, opportunity can knock at any time. Being prepared with such a simple tool is invaluable.

What would you say if you were asked right now, "So what is it that you do?" Please, never respond by saying that you are in "sales".

Your answer must be exciting and compel the prospect to act positively.

Here is the 30-second development process. It's simple and it works.

5 Seconds – Introduce yourself, your position, your company
10 Seconds – Creatively deliver 1-3 value propositions you offer
10 Seconds – Give a real example using percentages and related metrics
5 Seconds – Ask permission to contact the prospect

For example purposes, let's assume for a moment that you are at your cousin's wedding. You have strategically identified earlier during the day that you would like to get an appointment with your cousin. After all, he just acquired a construction business. You wait for the appropriate time and approach his table. You shake his hand, smile and say enthusiastically "Great to see you!"

Cousin: "Great to see you too, what are you up to these days?"

You: "Well Jim, I am with Johnson and Company here in New York with the Corporate Sales team. I am tasked with reaching out to corporations both large and small and developing opportunities within the construction industry. Are congratulations in order? I understand that you have recently acquired a construction company."

Cousin: "That's correct I most certainly did – Thank you."

You: "You know Jim; I just finished a very successful project with Adams Construction Company. We were able to reduce on site accidents by an additional 30% by implementing a very simple strategy that our company pioneered. In addition, they did not overspend their budget in doing so. In fact, the project was so successful, that we are now exploring other opportunities with two other affiliates next week. I realize that we are at a wedding, and we should not be talking business, however with your permission, may I exchange business cards with you right now, and get your permission to contact you by phone next week to set up an appointment to meet with you? I would really like the opportunity to meet you at your office."

Would you get the appointment? Sure, most likely; either in person or over the phone. In the end, the objective is to get to the next step – moving forward.

It would be advisable to work on a few versions until you come up with a great 30-second commercial. This absolutely will benefit you when you least expect it. Write it out, practice and rehearse it on video. Within hours, you will have a powerful commercial, which does not sound scripted or rehearsed in your toolbox.

The Sales Process

When you get to the core of selling, you begin to see a repetitive pattern develop in many of the things you do and say. There are certain things that happen that you can predict with certainty. For the most part, you will make the initial contact with the customer, meet with them, ask questions and make some kind of a proposal or presentation. At this stage, the customer will become a user or not. If they do, then there may be a series of steps that you or someone else must do to offer post sales support. If they didn't buy from you, you may have a step or series of steps that you will try in hopes of maintaining a relationship.

These predictable steps when defined become the company's sales process. They are there to guide the sale along. Doing so sets clear objectives of what is expected from the sales meeting and the company. By utilizing a sales process, you develop a common sales language, become better prepared for your meetings and remove unnecessary pressures on yourself during the sales process. It also allows you to be better prepared, relaxed and focused on meeting specific objectives that have been pre determined.

To make it easier for sales professionals, many companies employ electronic means to track the sales process of their representatives. Even the most seasoned sales professionals often struggle in grasping the real benefits of tracking the sale through its natural steps at the beginning. Unfortunately, many others overlook the benefits of tracking the sale as "extra work" or a "big brother tool" for sales managers to constantly look over their shoulder. Commonly, those who feel this way are either resistant to change and "of the old school", or are the happy underperformers on the sales team.

Pre-Call Plan

You will be amazed what 15 minutes on the Internet will provide you. Even knowing your customer's up to date stock price can build incredible value. Today, you can obtain information right on your cell phone.

For the most part, you only have between the hours of 8 and 5 to conduct your sales calls. In addition you must allocate time for travel, preparation and post sales commitments. Needless to say, managing your personal time is crucial.

Pre call preparation is one component in making your sales call meaningful to your client. Your customer dislikes it when you are not prepared for the meeting just as you don't like walking into a meeting that is meaningless; nobody does.

There is no reason today that you need to walk into a sales call unprepared. The Internet is a valuable resource for you. Company web sites are generally current and up to date.

Here is what information you should know before going into a sales call:

- ➢ Size of the company and scope
- ➢ Company Mission Statement
- ➢ Stock price and corporate news (if applicable)
- ➢ Customer's immediate competitors
- ➢ Customer's customer service policy
- ➢ Position and influence within industry

Accessing last minute and up to date information is available over your cell phone. Sales experts utilize these tools to keep themselves up to date with the latest knowledge.

When you arrive in a sales call prepared, you look like you're well versed and an industry expert. Customers like to talk about themselves. Asking them questions about themselves and latest company news is a great and professional way to begin any sales call. Customers will appreciate the opportunity that you give them, to talk about themselves or their company.

Pre call research also serves another reason: to gain the latest information and inspiration to formulate great questions. By doing so, your questions appear "customized" and specific to your customer's challenges, company and industry.

Beginning the Sale

Beginning the sales call is crucial. Remember, you have booked this meeting with the prospect. This is your meeting and just like being on time for the meeting, you are expected to begin the meeting.

One of the most embarrassing moments that could occur at this time is when your customer roles up his sleeves, leans forward and says, "...so what is this all about" or "...so what have you got for me?" This would not be good at all. To maintain control of the meeting, it is imperative you begin the meeting. Here is one of the most effective ways to begin the call. Simply begin by asking;

"Mr. Customer, is there any value in me introducing myself and my company first?"

An introductory question like this is extremely effective and safe as an opening line. It really does not matter what the answer is. If it is "yes", tell your 30-second commercial and end it with " ...and before I go any further, may I ask what it is that you do and how long have you been here?" Alternately, if the answer is no, simply ask the customer "Great, so where would you like to begin?"

You will also be calibrating for body language signs at this point. This is extremely important to realize. Observe how the customer sits, gestures and speaks when in a comfortable state. In a one-hour sales meeting, up to 700 different non-verbal cues can be transmitted by your customer.

Observe the customer's office for tell tale signs and demonstrate empathy, by mirroring the customer's tone and pace (rate of speech). Finally, you need to be observing the customer's behaviors and trying to identify their communication and personality styles as you both become engaged.

Questioning

In this book, we have allocated one entire chapter to asking great questions. That is how important this part of the sales process is. When you ask great questions, your customer sits up and takes notice. He regards you as the subject matter expert and listens to what you have to say.

Questioning your customer is a skill because your questions should be thought provoking and challenging the status quo.

Equally, you must learn to listen to the answers that you receive. You must read between the lines and resist the temptation to talk about everything that you offer (versus what your customer wants). Strategically, you will need to hold back specifics that don't address the customer's immediate needs. Reserve all the benefits you bring to the table for your final presentation.

Presenting

Now that you have effectively asked the right questions, gained all the information that you need, fully understand the fit that your company offers along with the benefits, it's time to create a sales presentation that makes sense.

Your presentation must be up beat and positive. When putting the program together, you must ask yourself these questions first.

Specifically, why should this customer deal with me? The answer should not be because I am a nice guy or I am the subject matter expert. That's what the other guys are saying. Your uniqueness should come from the meetings that you have had with the customer. By now they will have told you exactly what they expect of you that is different than the current supplier or vendor. The reason that the customer wants to deal with you can be different between your customers. Realize it and include it in your presentation.

Ask yourself specifically, what will your customer gain personally by going ahead with you after this presentation? There has to be a huge benefit for your prospect to change vendors or suppliers and go with you. Change management is a major issue with your customer and usually a critical deciding factor. What are you prepared to do to assist with this?

What other personal benefits will your customer receive by moving forward with you?

A couple of additional residual questions to ask are specifically, what benefits will your customer's division, department or team benefit by using you?

And finally, specifically, what benefits will the company gain by moving forward with you and your company?

Once again, these answers are custom to the feedback that you have received from your previous meetings. Dig deep and consider the root issues and benefits that you bring to the table.

Finally, list how many benefits the customer will gain by dropping the status quo and moving forward with you. This is where keeping great detailed notes for you to review will pay off. Once you have compiled your final list of key differentiators, make sure that each one is included somewhere in your presentation. Utilize subtle and direct approaches in your presentation to get your point across. Make sure that all the influencing points until now are included in your presentation.

Delivering your Presentation

If possible, practice your presentation in front of a peer or sales manager. If that is not possible to do, video tape yourself presenting your material. Obtaining feedback is critical to your overall success in sales. Remember this is your time to shine. You and your customer have invested a lot up to this point. Both of you have a lot at stake during the next meeting.

You will need to know exactly who will be in attendance for your presentation. You want to know the names and titles of each person. This information will allow you to prepare for a successful presentation. Sometimes this will remain between the two of you in their office. In other instances, you may be presenting to a panel or boardroom. Knowing who will be there will give you a good idea of what types of questions you may expect. If an operations manager is present, you can expect support and process based questions. If a VP of Finance is going to be present, you can expect finance related questions during or after your presentation.

179

Closing

This is going to be the shortest section in this chapter. That is because we are not interested in "slick" closes, gimmicks that trick the customer into becoming a user. Using the "puppy dog close" the "Ben Franklin close" and a multitude of other gimmick closes don't work like they used to.

Customers are smart. Customers look for people who can work together throughout the sales process so that the "close" is a natural piece of the overall picture. If you have completed all the steps together with your customer, the end should be a request to consummate the relationship.

Here is the "close" that is acceptable to use. After all is said and done, and your customer's questions are answered, then you are ready to proceed to the next step. That next step should be as simple as "Mr. Customer, this looks great to me, how about you?"

When they say yes – proceed.

If they say no – be sure to ask, "… other than that issue you just raised, is there anything else that you are concerned about?" Once all the objections are on the table, now it is time to address them one by one. Once you have addressed them satisfactorily, then repeat the "closing statement" once again.

Referrals

This is a critical step that is often overlooked by sales people. There seems to be a reluctance to ask for referrals yet it takes the least amount of effort on the part of the sales person. Sales people cite that it either makes them feel uncomfortable or they don't want to make the customer feel uncomfortable

Here's the reality. Accountants know other Accountants. CEO's know other CEO's. Sales Managers know other Sales Managers. Lawyers know other Lawyers and so on. This is powerful. It is important to realize that once you have had the opportunity to begin a relationship with one customer, they know others who will benefit from your product, service or offering.

Persuaders always ask for referrals and receive referrals. There are two types of referrals:

- ➢ Solicited Referrals
- ➢ Unsolicited Referrals

Solicited referrals are usually generated by asking the customer directly for the names of others who could benefit from your product, service or offering. Typically, they are a new or existing customer with significant knowledge or experience working with you or your company. Also, there may be instances where you have not been able to provide the right solution to a customer and they do not buy from you. It is perfectly acceptable to ask for a referral from the customer. After all, they are familiar with you and the solutions that you can provide.

Asking for a solicited referral usually comes at the end of the sales call. You will have a very clear indication if you were able to build trust and rapport with the customer. Your customer needs be sure that referring you to someone that they know, is going to be safe and that there are no negative repercussions as a result of doing so.

Solicited Referral Example:

"Mr. Prospect, now that we have come to the conclusion that there is a match (no match) between what we do, may I ask one additional favor?"

(Sure)

"My business is very dependent on reaching out to business professionals like you. I am sure that you demand the highest standard of professionalism from your sales team and management when they represent you and your company. Is that correct? "

(Yes)

"I would like to ask if I have met your criteria in both sales professionalism and demonstrated excellence in representing our company?"

(Yes)

"Then, with your permission, may I ask you to be kind enough to let me know who else comes to mind, that you could direct me to, who would benefit from my professionalism and product/service/ offering?"

(Hmm)

"Don't worry, most customers can think of only between 3-5 referrals when put on the spot like this. I greatly appreciate you doing this for me!"

Note: At this point, after the assumptive statement, do not utter another word. Resist the temptation to continue to speak. Allow as much time for your customer to think as necessary. You must master this skill. It is what gets you referrals on the spot versus, "Let me give it some thought. Can I email you one later on sometime?"

Unsolicited referrals are generated by someone who is familiar with your product service or offer. They may or may not be a direct result of something

181

that you have personally done in the past. For example, your company may have released a marketing campaign through various media and as a result, the prospect has called into your company and the lead was passed on to you. Subsequently, you could also receive a call from a prospect that was referred by an existing customer or user. These types of calls are usually unexpected and a welcome surprise.

Referrals are both gifts and rewards, usually for a job well done. Whenever you receive one, make sure to send a quick thank you note immediately, acknowledging receipt of the lead. It is equally important to let the referring party know when and how the opportunity has concluded. Communication is the key. The sales expert realizes that this simple gesture builds trust, respect and credibility with the referring party. He realizes that doing so only ensures a higher probability of additional gifts and rewards to come.

PART THREE:
THE SALES BRAND

Chapter Fifteen

Branding Yourself: The Art of Making YOU Unique

By this stage in your life you have undoubtedly discovered the power of brands. We all have our favorites. Do you need to have your Starbucks in the morning and no other coffee will do? Or maybe you run in your trusty Nikes and wouldn't entertain any other. How far out of your way would you drive to go to your favorite store?

We all identify with our brands. We even think of them as ours. For example, I love Mac computers. It doesn't matter to me if it costs more than using another kind of computer. I love Mac so much that if I'm working on my computer and feel the need to take a break, I will go to Apple's website and watch three or four Mac commercials. They make me feel so good that I'm refreshed and ready to get back to work. Why? Because I'm a Mac kind of guy.

Think about which brands are important to you. Do you go home after a hard day at work and put on you favorite pair of jeans? Maybe you stop by your favorite ice cream shop, take a drive in your dream car, or just plug in your iPod. Whatever your brands, they work for you. Maybe they wouldn't work for someone else, but they do for you. That is what branding is all about – you! When you identify with a brand it becomes a part of you. It brings you comfort and recharges your battery. You want more of it in your life.

You also want to share it with others. Brand power gets us excited and talking. Off the top of your head, what is your child's favorite restaurant? Where does your neighbor grocery shop? Maybe you even know where your co-worker buys books? Do they shop online (Amazon, Barnes & Noble or other) or like to go to the actual store (Borders, Barnes & Noble or that small independent bookstore in town)? It is one thing to know our favorite brands, but it's amazing how much we know about the favorite brands of others. This is because we all identify with *our* brands! They become a part of us. And we want to share them with others.

You see where I'm going with this, don't you? In our conversations with others we come to know their favorite brands. They spread the word. They preach the gospel of their favorite brands. They are the champions of their brands. Wouldn't you love to hear your clients champion you to those they talk with? When the need for your products or services arises do your clients think of you as the only person who can deliver? Do they think of you as the only one who can give them what they need at that moment? This is where you want to go. This is the power of branding YOU.

When thinking of my strongest brand loyalty, my mind goes directly to my Mac. I have a connection and it's a strong one. Over twenty-five years ago I sold a boat to buy my first Mac. It had only one megabyte of memory. No color. No Internet. Most applications were kept on separate disks. But I still loved it! Macs have improved over the years and these are some things I continue to identify with: the "ease of use" technology, the ability it gives me to express my creativity, the simplicity of its design and its attention to details. It feels like the people at Apple know me because they produce a product that speaks so well to my needs. The things that are important to me are important to Apple. All of these things make me a raving fan of Apple (could you tell?).

Wouldn't you love for your clients to have the same kind of emotion about you that I feel for my Mac? Do they talk to their friends about you? In their minds, have established yourself as "the only person that does what you do?" Let's talk more about how you can make this happen.

Branding YOU

Branding is about identifying and establishing you as a brand. This means in the eyes of your clients, you are the only person who does what you do.

The process of branding helps you move from defining yourself by your job title to a more specific position that you do better than anyone else. For example, with the power of branding, you can move from being an insurance agent (there are a lot of those) to being a Risk Eraser or a Wealth Protector or maybe even an Insurance Enthusiast. When you are good at what you do, this helps you become the only one who does what it is you do and does it right.

You see an Insurance Enthusiast does so much more than an insurance agent. If you are an Insurance Enthusiast, you make buying insurance fun! You give your clients an experience worth remembering and telling others about. You assume the responsibility for protecting their assets. You reduce their stress. You let them know that they don't have to know all the answers because you know insurance. You are the expert. As an Insurance Enthusiast, you are *enthusiastic* about insurance. You have a passion for it and it shows.

How cool would it be for one of your clients to tell a friend that they don't need an insurance agent? They have an Insurance Enthusiast to take care of all their risk. They pass along your card and say, "Forget about the stereotypical insurance salesmen. This lady is in a league of her own. She knows what she's doing and she loves everything about it. She'll take good care of you. Give her a call."

Poof!

Your competition just disappeared. In your client's mind, you are the only one who does what you do. When you are the expert and have a passion for your work you more quickly form your own brand. You become much more than a job title to your clients. Just like a Mac will always be more than just a computer to me.

This leads me to the piece of branding that is nearest and dearest to my heart. Using your passion to warp speed the formation of your brand.

The Power of Passion

In my opinion, one of the best compliments you can receive is to be told that someone admires your passion. Living with a passion for your work will help you to create "raving fans!" These are fans that tell others about you. This helps you get more referrals and produce more sales. That's the power of passion.

Passion is so personal to me. It has enabled me to succeed in situations in which I easily could have failed. This chapter shares a few stories about the role of passion in my life in hopes that these stories will spark your memories of those times in your life when passion was what carried you through to success. It ends with some tools to help you harness your passion to refuel your sales and more quickly establish the brand of YOU.

One of my earliest memories about the power of passion is of a service project I participated in as a twelve-year-old boy. Our church youth group was asked to take part in a service project to paint the home of an elderly woman in our community. My father took me to this project. He thought service was important and wanted me to learn how to share my talents and time with others. I, on the other hand, just wanted to get it over with so that I could go back to doing what twelve-year-olds like to do. I had no passion for the task at hand.

Not many twelve-year-olds would get too excited about giving up part of a Saturday to paint some old lady's house. Given I had little say in the matter, my plan was to do my part so that we could get the job done and go home. My assignment was to work in a room with a man named Cliff who was about my father's age - which of course made me think I couldn't possibly learn anything from him.

Cliff quickly got our materials together and then handed me a brush. We went to work. What started out as a "horrible day in my miserable life" (an attitude you can't fully appreciate until you have a twelve-year-old of your own) turned into a treasured memory. This memory shines even brighter with age.

As that day progressed, I noticed myself doing something I swore I would not do that day - smile. The longer I worked, the more I smiled. Why? What was happening? How could I betray myself by enjoying work? I knew better. If my father caught me having a good time then there would be more service projects in the future. My only hope of never being forced to give up another Saturday was to have such a horrible time that my father would never want to put us both through that misery again. But I couldn't help it. I felt like smiling!

187

Why? Cliff had passion! And it was contagious. He was smiling, joking, laughing and generally having a good time. I was completely confused. How could the world make sense if work equaled fun? Work meant the opposite of fun. Work meant drudgery. Work meant having anything *but* fun. And yet, there was Cliff, having FUN! And, so was I.

As we rode home that day, I actually found myself being pleasant. I was smiling, joking and talking (*with my dad* for heaven's sake). Disgusting! What was I thinking? What had happened to me? Had I been abducted and probed by aliens? Who was this nerd sitting next to my dad in the cab of his truck? I remember thinking, "I just might never forgive myself for this."

But from that moment on, I was sold on the power of passion. Cliff had "sold" me. He had changed my thinking. He had persuaded me to equate work with fun and I didn't even know that I was being sold. In the hundreds of projects I have served on since then, I have done them with a smile. Cliff's natural talent for living with passion had infected me. I found myself a fan of Cliff and a fan of passion. The power of passion changed a twelve-year-old's idea of work.

What can you learn from this story? Imagine, as a test of your ability to persuade, that your sales manager walks up to you with his twelve-year-old son. He says, "My son hates work (duh!) and I want you to persuade him that work is fun. Good luck." What would you do?

You say, "Hello, Mr. Twelve-year-old. My name is (insert name here). I am so excited about the opportunity to explain to you that work is fun! Have you ever had a job?"

Mr. Twelve-year-old says, "Dude! I'm twelve."

You say, "OK, but I assume that you do know what work is?"

Mr. Twelve-year-old says, "Dude! I'm twelve."

You say, "That's great, Mr. Twelve-year-old. Have you ever had fun?"

Mr. Twelve-year-old says, "Dude! I'm twelve."

You say, "OK, then let's go to lunch. That's fun! We can develop a rapport and get to know one another. We will then have a bond of trust on which to build our relationship."

Mr. Twelve-year-old says, "Dude! You're old. I am so outta here!"

And *you* are outta luck! In a situation like this, you need to bring some passion to the table quickly or you have lost.

To help think through how this conversation would look with passion, we can learn a lot by looking through the eyes of a child. Kids know how to have fun. Have you ever tried to teach a difficult task to a child? You probably were most successful by trying to make it fun. You had to figure out something creative so that you could engage the child in the task.

Say you wanted your son Jonathon to go to the end of the driveway and bring in the newspaper. Jonathon might stomp his feet and grumble, "Why do I have to do everything around here?" It's time to make a game out of it to help change your son's attitude. So the next time, you pull out a watch and say, "Jonathon, let's see how fast you can run to the end of the driveway, pick up the newspaper and run back here. Ready, set, go!" Off Jonathon goes, running as fast as he can. You just made it fun for him! He didn't mind getting the newspaper – he actually enjoyed getting the newspaper - because it was fun.

If you're not having fun in your work every day, you are not using your best talents. You also are not being YOU. Living with a passion helps us become creative in our jobs. We innovate more easily. We come up with new and exciting ways to serve our customers. They enjoy working with us. They even look forward to seeing us because they like being around such a positive influence.

Passion brings purpose to our work. When we have a purpose, we become more engaged. We focus on getting the job done. We no longer have the patience to sit around waiting for success to find us. Our minds are more open to inspiration. We find ourselves doing things that use our best talents and abilities. We become more authentic and it becomes easier to develop great relationships with our clients. Our sales move to a higher level because we are doing what we do best every day. We are living with a passion for sales.

When I was a Math Teacher, I sold my students on the fact that they could learn math. And selling, after all, is using our persuasive skills to help others understand how we can serve them. As a teacher, I learned how to use my passion for helping others to convince the students that I could help them learn how to do fractions. Once they were sold on the fact that *I could teach anyone fractions* they were able to relax and engage in a process of exploration. We would work together to find a way that they could understand math. It was fun! And that made all the difference in the world.

I started to receive referrals. The students who had passed my class would tell their friends (who also had trouble with math) to sign up for Mr. Adams' class. How is that for viral marketing at work? Remedial math soon became my niche and my classes were filled with students looking to achieve their first credit in math. It was fun and it was exciting. By simply finding my passion, my situation changed from hopelessness to renewed optimism. Now I encourage any young person with the desire to go into education to pursue it. What a great career!

Fast-forward a few years. Following my purpose had led me to a career as a financial advisor. This interest was developed while serving as the spokesperson for the teachers in bargaining a new contract. During negotiations, it became evident to me that most teachers were not adequately preparing for retirement. I could see how troubled some of the teachers' futures might be and I knew I needed to do something about it. I became a man with a mission to help my fellow teachers better prepare for retirement. This new purpose in life became my passion. I began working with the financial company that held a retirement savings plan for our district. My job was to work with teachers to help them save more for retirement.

Although this was my first professional sales position in the traditional sense, I had no doubt that I could use all of my selling skills that had been refined through 15 years of teaching. And it was true. I found myself in a similar situation to that of teaching fractions. Many of my clients hated finances and knew very little about investing for retirement. They were very busy people and it was difficult to get them to sit down and plan for their future. They were not interested in having another deduction taken out of their check.

Just like my former students, they gave countless excuses to not take the time to learn a difficult subject. "I don't understand things like investments." "My husband does the finances." "I'm too busy." "I've never understood this financial stuff and it's just so boring!" In order to overcome all of the excuses the teachers threw at me to not do something about their retirement, I used my passion as a tool.

As I let my passion show, I would say something like, "You do not need to like this financial stuff because I like it enough for the both of us." Or "Maybe you don't understand investing, but I do and I will help you understand." Of course I always started my conversations with a smile. This was easy to do because it was fun for me. I was excited to have the chance to change my clients' future for the better. If I could get them to take action, it meant that they would have a larger nest egg when it came time to retire. I was doing work that mattered.

The teachers would make comments like, "Well, I can see you have a passion for this." This confirmed that I was on the right track. When they saw my passion for managing their finances, they were more willing to talk about the details of their financial life and planning for their future. They became more comfortable about relying on my advice to make decisions. Because my clients were now engaged in the process of planning for their future, they were motivated to take action. Even if it was a small start, at least they got started. They also realized the importance of sitting down with me on an annual basis to review their plan. During the annual review, there would be more decisions made, which led to more sales.

My passion for sales changed the way my clients talked about me. Instead of saying, "Look out, the investment guy is in the lounge today," they would talk about a helpful conversation we had or how good they felt that they now were doing something about their future. Some clients would take another teacher by the hand and walk them down to see me as they said, "You need to talk this guy. You need to start saving for your retirement." Now, how fun is that? Clients bringing in new clients!

Pursuing Your Passion

I hope my personal stories help bring to life for you the power of passion! Passion changes everything. If you're not passionate about your work then why should your clients be? How can you expect your clients to become engaged with you if you have no passion for your job?

It's time to embrace your passion. Following are a few simple tools to use to help yourself ignite your passion.

Create an "I believe" list

Start by making an "I believe..." list. Write down the things you believe to be true about your work and life. Think about the values that drive you, the principles you wish to live by and the things that matter to you. For example, "I believe it's important to be positive in life" or "I believe in making others better for having knowing me."

What do you believe about your current job? "I believe my job is important because ..." Why does doing what you do matter? Fill in the missing words. This process will help you to remember who you are and who you want to become. It's energizing to remember the things we believe. After you complete a list about your job, make a list for other areas of your life that are important to you.

When you finish your "I believe" list, keep it in a place where you can review it every day. Add or delete beliefs as you grow. The purpose of this list is to help you become more authentic. To move in the direction of the person you want to become.

As we think about the things that we truly believe - the values and principles we wish to live by - we remember who it is we want to become. This process helps us recommit to becoming that person. It keeps us on track when things happen in life that could move us away from our core beliefs. It can provide inspiration and help us think about ways we want to act in the future to become a better version of ourselves. These ideas and moments of inspiration can tell us what action we should take next. Don't let these thoughts pass by without recording them.

Listen for inspiration

After you have created your "I believe" list, the next step is to keep an "Inspiration Log." Use whatever type of notebook that will be easy for you to keep with you. It can be paper, electronic, large or small - whatever fits your style.

Whenever an idea pops into your head, write it down. These ideas are gifts. Many times, if implemented, they will take us to the next level. If you don't write these ideas down as they come to you, after a while you will forget about them. Have you ever seen a new product or a new sales system and thought, "That's my idea! I thought of that! They stole my idea!"? Well, they didn't steal your idea. They recorded and acted upon one of their own ideas. This brings us to the next step. You've got to act!

Take daily action

Review your inspiration log daily and choose some action to take. Today. The action doesn't have to be big. It just has to be today.

Some times we convince ourselves that we can't take any action until we know the whole plan. We want to know how our action today is going to lead to success in the future. We decide to wait until we develop the entire plan first. When that complete plan just doesn't come together, we end up not taking any action at all.

Do you tend to wait to see how things are going to work out before taking action? Is it because without all of the details you think you might fail? The fear of failure is paralyzing. We are afraid to look stupid or have someone judge our actions as foolish. The sad part is that when we see others who have brought our ideas to fruition, we call them lucky. "How can she be so lucky? It was my idea." It wasn't luck. That person merely acted upon the inspiration she received.

A while back I heard a story about driving a car at night. The story points out that even though the lights of a car only shine about 100 yards or so in front of us we can drive clear across the country. When we get into our car, we can't see our final destination. But by illuminating 100 yards at a time, we can safely arrive. Don't wait for something that will probably never happen. You won't know the full plan. Take action anyway.

Can you see how these "Pursuing Your Passion" tools work together? Let's review them.

Make an "I believe..." List

Write down the things that you believe to be true. Think of the values and principles you wish to live by. Think about the person you want to become. Read your list every day. By knowing who you are, you will open yourself up to new sources inspiration on how to become even more of what you believe.

Keep an Inspiration Log

You will be surrounded by ideas and moments of inspiration about what it is you should do next in order to become the best version of yourself. Write down these ideas as they come to you in your Inspiration Log. We all get great ideas from time to time and we forget most of them because we never write them down. Keep an inspiration log to record all of your great ideas.

Take action every day!

When we record ideas and inspirations, we have a whole list of possible daily actions. Commit to picking one idea and taking some action every day. This will bring you closer to your destination. Remember that you don't need to see the whole picture or know with certainty that everything will work out. You only need to see just far enough to take some action that will get you to the next point of inspiration. Then, you can take another action, which will lead to even more action.

As you are reading this chapter you might have an idea pop into your head. That is inspiration. Start your inspiration log right now. Write down the ideas that are floating around in your head. Then take some kind of action on one of these ideas.

Here is an example of how easy this can be. While I was writing this chapter the idea of making myself a T-shirt to remind myself how important passion is popped into my head. I got online and Googled T-shirt. I found a place where I could design and order a T-shirt. My new "Got Passion?" T-shirt will arrive in 3 to 5 days. Easy! This is one little action that will help me stay on course and keep passion a part of my life. Remember that your action doesn't need to be *big*. It just has to be today!

These tools will help you become engaged in your own success. When you start to live by the principles and values that you believe to be true, you will start to become the person you want to be. You will become a better version of yourself. You will find yourself taking actions that come from inspiration. You won't be able to hide your passion because you will know what it is that you should be doing. You will embrace each day as an opportunity to do what you do best. You will become passionate about your work.

Put the power of passion to work for you to better serve your clients. Increase your referrals and your sales by having a passion for what you do. Passion gives you fans! Passion gets people talking. Your fans will talk about you to their friends. When you do what you do best, you will have more fun, get more done and make more sales. That is the power of passion!

Branding and passion go hand in hand. You get to do what you do best every day. You get to serve your clients using your best talents and abilities. You put this into words and form a brand that tells others what you do better than anyone else. Your clients will love working with you and they will tell their friends about you. You are now so much more than a job title. You have your own brand. That is the power of passion. Put it to work to brand YOU!

PART FOUR:
SALES MANAGEMENT

Chapter Sixteen

So You Want to Be A Sales Manager?

Many successful organizations promote from within the company. This is a very powerful and positive motivator for all employees. Companies have a large investment in every employee that they hire. There are both hard and soft costs associated with employee retention and churn. Grooming existing employees into leadership positions has many benefits to any employer. Promoting from within the company demonstrates to everyone that there are opportunities for career advancement and develops a sound culture.

There may be an instance during your career when you may be asking yourself, "What is it that I would like to do next in my career in sales?"

In some instances it may be the aspiration to migrate from inbound sales to outbound sales. Some may like the opportunity to move into larger account sales within the corporate sales team while others would like to get into a leadership or management position.

One of the benefits of sales is that it does open up a variety of opportunities from a career development perspective. After all, selling is a position that involves people interaction. We develop great communication skills, personal time management skills and conflict resolution skills. Although these are great attributes to take with you into any management position, there are many additional skills to leading people that you need to know.

This chapter is intended to shed some light on the similarities and differences of sales and sales management that you will want to consider while still selling. These secrets are intended to expose some of the skills that you should be developing right now in preparation of achieving your career goal, if becoming a sales manager is in your long or short term plan.

Quite often, sales managers are promoted based on a job well done in selling. For a VP of Sales, Director of Sales or even an exiting sales manager, it is a very logical place to look first. Senior leaders will almost always look into what bench strength they have before going outside to recruit a new sales manager. It is cost effective and efficient from many perspectives for the senior leaders to do so. This is your first advantage over anyone else being considered.

Senior executives will often demand from their leadership team that they begin to develop succession plans for their replacements. While a sales manager, I recall being mandated to have at least two people earmarked for succession planning. As a matter of fact, it became such a focal point of interest to the executive team that it was brought up on the agenda as a discussion point every eight weeks with the VP of Sales. This ensured that it remained a top priority in our minds. This helped all of the sales managers to constantly observe and help everyone who demonstrated leadership qualities of a potential successor. This put a real emphasis to covertly begin to develop the necessary skills, which were identified as a required development, for promotion within the organization.

There are several examples where top producing sales people are not properly prepared for the new position of sales manager. In many instances, getting the promotion is like being handed a recognition award for a job well done. I have seen this happen many times and have coached many sales managers who express regret that they left sales and migrated into management. Often there is a "buyer's remorse" which kicks in. Usually, around six months into the new role, when the new dose of reality sets in, many begin to question if the decision to leave sales was in fact the best decision for them.

So what has happened between the time that the manager left sales and entered the leadership position? After all, the sales person was hired because someone in senior management thought that they could *do* the job. The sales person, who accepted the promotion, did so because they thought that they could *do* the job.

The main reason why promoted sales people struggle, and often fail, at managing people begins with the lack of preparedness that is required and continues when the required training and development are lacking, leading up to the new role. Many of these skills need to be honed and developed while still selling. Managing people is not as easy as it seems on the surface. Leaders are not born, they are developed.

The company isn't at fault for hiring you into the sales manager's position. This is the ultimate demonstration of trust as they openly include you in the big picture and the long-term vision of the organization. Where many companies drop the ball however, is during the grooming stage. They are quick to pull the trigger and promote someone who is not quite ready to do the job. The best intentions are there, but the timing is off and skills necessary to do the job are not quite mature.

Helping Others

Prior to making the transition into sales management, begin to think of all those things that you would change for the better if you had the authority to do so as a sales manager. Begin to think of all the challenges that you would like to overcome if you had a magic wand. Write each point down and promise to yourself that you won't duplicate it. This is the first step to ensure that your ego remains in check when you do receive a promotion.

Remember, in many cases, the very people that you will be asked to support in the new role are your peers today. Gaining respect and trust from them now

198

will go a long way later. Begin to demonstrate a willingness to help. Show your current sales manager that you are willing to help.

Offer your time to shadow others on sales calls. Ask to lead a sales meeting or at the very least present something of value to everyone. Offer to take a new account manager under your wing. These offers of assistance do not go unnoticed. You will gain valuable hands on experience as to the responsibility of leading people. Additionally, you are sending the signal to your current management team that you are ready to accept additional responsibilities.

Personal Recognition

It is no secret that in sales, being recognized and rewarded by customers, peers and management is pinnacle to our overall motivation and performance. The best form of recognition from our customer is when we get an unsolicited referral. This demonstration of trust and confidence in you cannot be bought. This is proof that you have brought value to your customer by demonstrating superior customer service and your solution is value added.

When we are recognized by our companies, once again, it is usually for a job well done. We have met or exceeded a sales forecast, target or quota and thus have qualified for a reward. We can win small tokens of appreciation such as gift certificates and movie tickets, which are typical of short contests, usually a monthly or quarterly program.

Larger rewards such as annual sales trips and memberships into the president's club are in place for the long term. They serve two purposes. First, it helps the sales team focus on a long term objective and sales target. This benefits the company in achieving their commitments and promises to investors, stakeholders and shareholders. Finally, long-term incentives reduce involuntary rep churn within an organization.

Being a part of so many opportunities and often being on a pedestal, makes it difficult to take a back seat to all that glory.

When managing people, it is all about recognizing others. You will be creating the incentive programs for others. You will be giving the recognition to others and you will not be participating in the incentives that allow you to earn more money intermittently. Because of this, many new sales managers experience a surprising drop in their income as well. In many cases, you will be taking on more responsibility and earning less money.

When looking to move up into a management career, think through the possibility that this may indeed be the case with you.

Expected Changes

When asking sales people, "Who is your competition", many will begin to name the different companies with whom they directly compete against as a service provider. Others will state that the real competition is the status quo – the current state of what the customer does and how he does it.

Daily, in sales, the battle takes place "out there" in the trenches, driving to and from the customer's office, battling traffic and putting up with the attitude of the general public. Arriving at the office for some sales persons becomes a haven of rest from the ongoing responsibilities out in the field.

As a sales person, you are also accustomed to the liberty of movement. You are encouraged to be in the field and getting face time with your customers. You come in and out of the office as your schedule and appointments demand. Your activity begins to dictate your personal management of time.

As a sales manager, many of your liberties that you are accustomed to when selling are interrupted. Suddenly, you are required to be in the office, accessible to the entire team. Naturally, there are times when you are in meetings however your main customer is now the entire sales team. The demand on your time will not allow you to become a phantom or absentee manager. When issues need to be addressed, you must be available by email, phone and in person.

Your customer base has also increased. Instead of managing your own portfolio, you become responsible for everyone's as well. This responsibility can be overwhelming for many new managers because the sales people will always feel that their issue is a priority.

To gain a better appreciation for what it is like to be juggling these concerns, pay close attention to your current sales manager as he deals with the daily affairs. Observe how he deals with each situation. Then multiply what you see tenfold.

Here's a method by which your sales manager could use your help. The next time that you have a problem which requires your sales manager's input and decision, always be prepared to offer a viable solution. This is the best way that you can demonstrate to your current manager that you are thinking through the issue. Quite often, just taking the time for a moment to think the issue through, resolves the matter without the interaction of a manager. Let your current sales manager realize that you are a problem solver.

Don't Stop Selling

A sales manager is the representative and spokesperson on behalf of the entire team. Internally, they are responsible for raising the profile with other managers and leaders within the company. Occasionally, conflicts can arise between departments and it is left up to the managers to sort out the issues. Sometimes these issues can escalate and conflicts do arise. In every organization, the sales manager and VP of Sales are competing and negotiating with other departments for budgets, finances, headcount, marketing and training.

Remember, sales managers still have to maintain contact with customers. Often, they are asked to intervene during the sales process to help close a sale. They get involved and help mediate customer's issues as they arise. Sales managers will negotiate more deals and have to make more decisions than sales people who sell every day.

Being a superior negotiator and diplomat will go a long way when you become a manager. Mastering superior communication and negotiating skills now will be extremely beneficial when you finally get your promotion to manage a sales team.

Get Started Now

As you seriously consider getting into a leadership role as part of your career aspirations, talk to someone in a management role that you are comfortable with.

Find a mentor who you feel is a superior leader and someone that you would like to emulate. Identify what skills you would like to develop. Ask for feedback from those that you trust and are honest with you.

Let your sales manager know that you are ready for the next step and you would like to work on a career development plan.

This is the quickest way to gain insight and knowledge into what it takes to become a great leader.

Chapter Seventeen

Sales Management Secrets

Demonstrating Leadership

There are two types of leaders; those that are leader breeders and those that are leader blockers. This is dependent on personal agenda and the competency of the leader.

When a leader is closed minded, looking over their shoulder, paranoid and disorganized, they are leader blockers. They are always concerned and worried about others becoming a threat to their position, responsibility and career. They seem confused and waver between thoughts and second-guess their decisions. A leader in this capacity and mindset can prove to be harmful to any sales organization. When an organization experiences a high volume of sales rep churn, quite often it may be due to a poor manager who is not an effective communicator and motivator.

Leader breeders are experts in bringing out the best in others. They put the primary focus on the development and success of others first. They are confident, demonstrate resourcefulness and are always willing to help. Great leaders are always willing to invest in their own personal development and are always willing to share that valuable information. Great leaders demonstrate empathy, trust, and knowledge. They are respectful of their own responsibilities and that of others around them. Great leaders are masters at ethically motivating and persuading others to achieve the best in both the personal and business lives of their teams.

Leadership Characteristics

Great leaders are effective communicators. They strive to share information with their sales people and then go out and learn some more. They have the knack of truly understanding what motivates each person. They recognize that they cannot walk in with a "cookie cutter approach" to motivating people.

If you are familiar with the National Football League in the USA, then you will have heard of the head coach of the Seattle Seahawks, Mike Holmgren. Coach Holmgren has a long list of accomplishments. He has lead two different

203

football teams to the Superbowl and won the championship once. He has taken both teams that he coached from losing seasons to post season play. Teams that couldn't win games suddenly were regarded as top contenders. Here is a guy who dealt with well-paid athletes who have some very large egos. How could he possibly have led two different teams to such great success?

It was during the 40th Superbowl when the Seattle Seahawks lost the Superbowl to the Pittsburgh Steelers. Coach Holmgren was being interviewed after the loss to the Steelers. The reporter asked how it was possible to be so successful in turning football teams around.

Coach Holmgren cited that first he had to figure out how his players like to communicate. Then he had to figure out what motivated them and finally he made sure that they were paid well.

Great sales managers realize the importance of figuring out exactly what each sales person's preferred communication style is. This can be determined by understanding what personality type the individual is. Both are directly linked to each other.

The Myers-Briggs Type Indicator is a powerful tool for any sales manager to use. There are many other tools available which identify personality types accurately as well. Successful sales managers utilize these tools to identify what type of communication style the sales person prefers. Once this has been accomplished the sales manager can modify their communication style to match that of the sales person.

Knowing what motivates each sales person will identify how to keep them inspired. Some people are motivated by the carrot and some by the stick. Do they repel from fears and gravitate towards rewards? What are the personal, long and short-term goals of the sales person? Great sales managers understand each sales person's key drivers and help the individual accomplish those goals. Understanding what motivates a sales person allows the sales manager to customize a game plan for success.

Effective Sales Meetings

There are two very important questions that you should be asking yourself when it comes to the effectiveness of your sales meetings. It's important to go into the past and recall when you were selling. Empathize as one of the attendees and then ask yourself "How would I rank my last sales meeting and am I looking forward to next week's meeting?"

Your answer must be a definite and unconditional "yes" and "yes". If you had to think about it or you answered anything but yes, then you have some work to do.

I was asked to sit in on a Monday morning sales meeting. I was invited in by the VP of Sales and the sales manager to speak about motivation and pump up the troops. Morale was low and the fourth quarter was fast approaching. The fourth quarter was the busiest quarter for sales.

These scheduled meetings occurred every Monday at 9:00 am. I arrived early and was sitting in the boardroom when one by one; the sales team began to arrive. I recall introducing myself to everyone and then the meeting was called to order. It was 9:10. I observed the body language of the sales team sitting around the very large boardroom table. Fifteen sales professionals, nobody smiling, shoulders slumped, leaning back in their chairs, pens tapping, arms and legs crossed and absolutely nobody was smiling. This team would have found more pleasure watching paint dry on a wall in Las Vegas during the month of July.

Just as I was expecting a great opening remark from the sales manager to set the tone and get everyone engaged, the sales manager blurts out, "So, let's go around the table and hear from everyone what went wrong last week?"
I couldn't believe my ears. Asking a loaded question like that was devastating to everyone there. No wonder they were dejected and disengaged. Every Monday morning turned into a finger pointing and blaming exercise. How could this benefit the sales team and set the tone for the rest of the week for everyone to be productive?

After the sales meeting, the sales manager and I continued our meeting once everyone had left. The sales manager asked me what I thought. I threw the question right back and asked for his opinion first. He went on about all the challenges that the team was experiencing with operations and the back end support. He began to echo all the same points that the sales people raised for the last hour.

I questioned how long these issues had been going on. He said, "Oh, a couple of months now."

I asked, "Has there been any progress at all in improving the current system?" He replied, "Not really. The operations manager is very uncooperative and unwilling to change anything."

I asked, "Why?"

He answered that it was because the sales people were far too demanding on his staff. He went on to say that there really wasn't much more that he could do about it. In other words, he was willing to let it go on forever.

In the end, it was an issue that became personal between the two managers. They were unable to look past their own egos and look at the bigger picture. Everyone suffered including the customer, company and both teams, who were forced to battle each other.

This internal conflict had escalated to be the agenda item for the sales team every Monday morning. There is no reason that something this severe should go on for this long. Within two 1 hour mediated meetings, everything was worked out. All they needed to do was redefine the current policies to meet the demand due to a steady increase in sales.

Sales people, like most of us, want to see results. Issues that are not resolved at the managerial level from one week to the next, sends a clear message that there is no one supporting them. If the issue requires time to be resolved, then you must always provide a recap at your sales meetings outlining the progress that has been accomplished since the last meeting.

There must always be some forward progress to the issues raised at the previous meeting.

Show your team that you are there for them. Let them know that you will support them when they need it.

Punctuality

Being punctual for any meeting is something that is assumed and expected. A team sales meeting is no different than an appointment with your most important customer. Nobody should be late as it is disrespectful to everyone who has made it to the meeting on time.

Beginning the sales meeting on time is also very important. It sets a great example to everyone that all meetings within your control should begin as scheduled.

Finally, it is also important to conclude the meeting on time. This allows the sales people to have the ability to manage their personal time effectively.

Preparation

Being prepared for your team is the first key to a successful meeting. Your sales meeting should be no more than one hour in length and should be structured. When the meeting is structured, it has meaning, purpose and direction.

Having an agenda to lead the meeting allows everyone involved to realize what important issues will be addressed. This can be as simple as a short email outlining both the content and the duration of time allocated to each item.

In addition, you should treat your sales meeting with the same preparedness and attention as you did prior to your most important sales presentation. You need to have a purpose and an objective. Just like your most important sales call, you are constantly building trust, demonstrating knowledge and exhibiting passion for what you do.

Allocate the time throughout the week to be strategic in what you hope to accomplish. Demonstrate to your new team that you are investing time in them. Strategically bring forward only those issues that will bring value to everyone. Addressing concerns, which affect a couple of people, should be addressed in another meeting. Don't bring forward petty items like process changes, policy changes or internal events and calendars. These things can be addressed through a simple email.

Try to plan out a strategy for your sales team which coincides with major events or corporate objectives. If in three weeks you are aware of a major marketing initiative profiling a specific product, then you need to ensure that your team is prepared and ready to deliver results quickly. You may consider dedicating a small amount of time from your agenda to address any shortfalls that you may anticipate. Great managers solicit feedback from the sales teams and generate dialogue, which bring forward ideas and strategies. Questions like "What do you think about..." and "What would you guys suggest..." are terrific generating ideas collectively.

Don't present and do all the talking. Involve your sales team and get them talking. Sales people need to be recognized as contributors and change agents. In the end, just ask yourself, "Did this meeting bring any value to them?"

Inspiration

Keeping your meetings inspirational make sales people want to attend. This is a golden opportunity to get everyone excited and enthusiastic about what they do. Don't bring negativity into your meetings. Never open up with loaded questions that fill the entire meeting with negativity. Keep the meetings light and engaging. Fun meetings are those that people look forward to. Keep in mind that just because a meeting is light doesn't mean that it is non- productive, meaningless and of no value.

Always look for a story to form around a theme. If a sales person was able to overcome a major obstacle on a specific account utilizing a creative strategy, make it a theme. Ask the sales person to share their success with the rest of the team at the next sales meeting. Be sure to recognize the accomplishment publicly.

Bring humor into your meetings. Everyone loves to laugh. Keep the pace of the meeting moving. Don't dwell and debate issues that have no hope of resolution and breed negativity. Stick to the agenda. If there is time left over, revisit the issue if you feel it is warranted.

Bring value to your meetings and utilize the collective brainpower of your sales team. Develop strategies to market, incentive and marketing programs as well as any other event that can lever input from everyone.

Remember to leave on a high note. Leave everyone wanting to come back for more. Be known for having great inspirational and productive meetings.

Incentives and Recognition

Great managers don't forget how much recognition meant to them when they were selling. They use the sales meeting as a platform to share the successes in front of fellow selling peers. A simple congratulatory comment expressed in the presence of others goes a long way. Inviting senior leaders to sales meetings is also a great strategy to inspire the individual and the entire team.

Simply sending out a congratulatory email to a sales person recognizing a job well done will go a long way. Copying the rest of the sales team including a member of the senior leadership team is a strategic, simple and effective way to motivate and inspire any sales person even more.

Great leaders realize the impact of recognition on their sales team. Selling is about momentum. Highly effective sales managers realize this and seek out help in maintaining momentum throughout the year.

The development of incentive programs is one of the ways to help accomplish this. These programs are generally designed to drive a certain behavior or achieve a certain performance target. It isn't uncommon to see more than one incentive program running parallel to each other throughout the year.

Sales organizations will generally have an annual program that is intended to deliver long-term performance results and reduce churn among the sales team members. These programs are usually larger in value and recognize the elite sales professionals who exceed their performance targets.

It would not be uncommon to have awards with exclusive titles such as "President's Council" or "Top 5% Club". Generally, the monetary value of these awards is higher and can consist of multiple smaller awards such as an annual trip for two, spending money, a briefcase and an exclusive logo on the business card. These programs typically involve other internal departments like marketing and require the sponsorship of the senior management team. Great sales managers will use these annual programs effectively to generate and maintain sales momentum of their team.

Shorter-term incentive programs are designed to deliver instant results or change behavior within the sales team – quickly.

For instance, a sales manager who identifies an immediate need to generate activity for the upcoming sales quarter, may offer a ten dollar gas card for the first person who books three new first appointments on the phone.

The incentive is there to generate activity.

Shorter programs are typically left up to the sales manager's discretion to create and implement. Effective sales managers are experts at developing incentive programs which are effective motivators and achievable by everyone on the sales team.

Investing In Your People

Personal development is pinnacle in maintaining the skills necessary for your sales team to compete in the real world. As a manager, you need to look at various options available to ensure that your sales goals are going to be met.

Your sales targets increase year after year. As a manager, you are ultimately responsible for these deliverables.

Identifying training requirements that develop specific skills of team members is a sign of a great leader. Observation of newly formed habits and changes in behavior within the sales team is a sign of an alert manager. Acting quickly to address identified needs builds trust and credibility. It also demonstrates to everyone that you are proactive in keeping the team focused on selling and meeting the overall objectives.

Personal development can be accomplished in many different ways and can accommodate any training budget. The investment in everyone's personal time can range from one half hour to a full day.

Great managers do not view personal development as a cost, but rather an investment. No matter what your training budget is, you can always deliver a great program to help your team develop any area of concern.

Having a senior member of the leadership team such as the President, CEO, V.P or Director address your sales team is extremely powerful. Most senior executives will invest their time to speak with sales people. They lend credibility and can address a variety of topics such as corporate policy, direction, opportunities, culture and competition. Be prepared, give them plenty of notice and be specific as to what goal you are trying to accomplish.

You would be surprised as to how receptive your customers are towards coming into a sales meeting to address your team. Customers can be instrumental in sharing inside knowledge of how your product and service benefits them on a daily basis and what was the decision making criteria. Your investment is usually a lunch and the overall benefit is invaluable to your sales team.

Manufacturers' reps, suppliers and distributors are perfect resources to tap into. Invite the representative to address your team on the latest products, services, applications and success stories that others have experienced. They are also very receptive to bringing in corporate items such as jackets and shirts, which can be used as an incentive during the meeting.

A formal presentation delivered by a peer is a great method to deliver a message. It is unique and powerful. Sales people can share specific information relating to sales tactics and techniques. In addition, they can be asked to demonstrate specific skills or reveal useful resources, which will prove beneficial to others.

Developing a library of resources within the branch office is another great strategy. Collectively, most sales people have favorite books and tools that they use on a regular basis. CDs, DVDs and audio programs are readily available. Utilize the Internet and join various mailing lists of training specialists and authors who have programs and free information available to assist in the development of your own training module.

Specialized third party sales training companies are an excellent way to deliver effective and specific skills training to any sales team. The benefit of these companies is that they are specialized in the skills that they address. You can find training companies that specialize in specific skills such as body language, influence, persuasion, prospecting, and negotiating to name only a few. Utilizing a specialized training company is cost effective and an excellent program can suit any training budget.

Great sales managers are effective communicators, motivators and leaders who are willing to help develop the skills necessary for sales people to become successful. Being attentive and resourceful to the team is invaluable in demonstrating your leadership qualities. Invest in them and invest in yourself.

Chapter Eighteen

The Close

Implementation is everything. Money follows action.

That is a phrase I have people repeat whenever they see me at a live event. And, I'd like to have you repeat it with me now. Go ahead.

"Implementation is everything. Money follows action."

Now repeat it out loud.

I want you to get comfortable with this idea because it is one of the basic truisms of improving your ability to sell.

An old saying that people like to repeat is that knowledge is power. But it isn't. *Applied* knowledge is power and that is what "implementation is everything" means. You must apply the lessons you've learned. You must evolve the core message to fit your circumstance. No one can do it for you; you have to do it for yourself. High Achievers and Top Earners do it relentlessly and you have to as well because when you do, the money follows.

You've just invested some quality learning time in improving your selling career. You've just learned lessons from seasoned sales professionals that when applied will take your career and your life to the next level no matter where you are today.

My suggestion is to go back through the book a chapter at a time and focus on implementing one the key ideas in one chapter for at least seven days. You don't have to do the chapters in order; in fact I recommend that you don't.

Grab a piece of paper right now and outline the key points of the chapter in the book that most resonated with you, the one that made the whole book worth reading. I want you to not only list the ideas that you'll implement, but I want you to write down how and where you'll implement them. And, I want you to write down how you'll know you've been successful in the implementation. Glenn Dietzel, a very wise man, says that "Writing is the doing part of thinking."

One of the biggest challenges I see in learning new tasks is that the person learning it can't describe success. If you can't describe how you'll know you've been successful in the application of the new knowledge, how will you ever know when to move on to the next thing?

Internalize these ideas; make them a core part of who you are. Review your outline every day, the moment you sit down to work, just before you go to lunch, the moment you return and just before you leave in the evening.

By writing what is important for you and taking action, you create a powerful new set of possibilities by using your new tools.

To succeed you must create focused time for action. Do that now. Literally make an appointment in your calendar once a week for the next 12 months to take action on something new that you are learning or implementing.

Michael Gerber has great advice for business owners – he says to spend more time working on your business not in your business. That advice applies to salespeople as well. Don't spend all your time working in your sales capacity, mark out specific time to work on you and your sales ability. That focused time spent learning and implementing is one of the most definable differences between the consistent six figure salespeople and everyone else.

Invest your time, energy and focus in you and on you.

In sales the close is all about bringing everyone around to the most obvious conclusion . . . the one you present. In a book, the close is about bringing you around to leveraging one or two simple ideas.

I hope you've listed your two or three most important ideas from this book and are ready to put them into play.

Because . . .

Implementation is everything. Money follows action.

And I know you are an Action Taker!

Bibliography

Beck, Martha. *Finding Your Own North Star: Claiming the Life You Were Meant to Live*. New York: Three Rivers Press, 1992.

Buckingham, Marcus, and Curt Coffman. *First Break All the Rules*. New York: Simon & Schuster, 1999.

Buckingham, Marcus, and Donald Clifton. *Now, Discover Your Strengths*. New York: The Free Press, 2001.

Cherry, Paul. *Questions That Sell*. AMACOM, 2006.

Collins, Jim C. *Good to Great*. New York: HarperCollins, 2001.

Covey, Stephen R. *The 7 Habits of Highly Effective People*. New York: Simon & Schuster, 1989.

Covey, S., et al. *First Things First*. New York: Fireside, 1994.

Csikszentmihalyi, Mihaly. *Flow*. New York: HarperPerennial, 1990.

GALLUP MANAGEMENT JOURNAL. 2007.

http://gmj.gallup.com/default.aspx

Gee, Val, and Jeff Gee. *Open Question Selling*. McGraw-Hill, 2007.

Gitomer, Jeffrey. *The Sales Bible, the Ultimate Sales Resource*. Hoboken: John Wiley & Sons, Inc., 2003.

Godin, Seth. 2007. *The Dip*. New York: Penguin Group.

Groppel, Jack L., and Bob Andelman. *The Corporate Athlete: How to Achieve Maximal Performance in Business and Life*. Hoboken: Wiley, 1999.

Gschwandtner, Gerhard. *The Ultimate Sales Training Workshop*. McGraw-Hill, 2007.

Hogan, Kevin. *The Psychology of Persuasion - How to Persuade Others to Your Way of Thinking*. Gretna: Pelican Company, Inc., 1996.

Klymshyn, John. *The Ultimate Sales Managers' Guide*. Hoboken: John Wiley & Sons, Inc., 2006.

Loehr, James E., *Stress for Success*. New York: Times Business, 1997.

Loehr, Jim and Tony Schwartz, *The Power of Full Engagement*. New York: Simon & Schuster, 2003.

Lakhani, Dave. *Persuasion, the Art of Getting What You Want*. Hoboken: John Wiley & Sons, Inc., 2005.

Monster.Com. *Monster Career Advice*. Article: "What Are Your Greatest Strengths and Weaknesses?" 2007

Peters, Tom. *Re-imagine!* London: Dorling Kindersley Limited, 2003.

Smith, Benson and Tony Rutigliano. *Discover Your Sales Strengths: How the Worlds Greatest Salespeople Develop Winning Careers*. New York: Warner Business Books, 2003.

Suls, J., Martin, R., & Wheeler, L. "Social Comparison: Why, with whom and with what effect?" *Current Directions in Psychological Science*, 11 2002: 159-163.

Vickers, Michael. *Becoming Preferred - How to Outsell Your Competition.* Englewood: Summit P, 2002.

Ziglar, Zig. *Selling 101*. Nashville: Thomas Nelson, Inc., 2003.

Meet the Authors

Larry Kevin Adams is **The ACTIONATOR!**

Using a three-step program to move your organization to embrace a culture of ACTION, **The Actionator** brings high impact solutions to employee engagement. Larry Kevin shows you how to use **ASK – LISTEN – ACT** to become a real live ACTIONATOR! How can you rise to the top of your sales team? TAKE INSPIRED ACTION! How can your team become the best in your organization? TAKE INSPIRED ACTION! How can your organization move into the ranks of exceptional? TAKE INSPIRED ACTION!

Larry Kevin works with individuals, teams, and organizations to engage them in "work that matters". Taking on a culture of ACTION is not always easy but necessary to become exceptional. An ACTIONATOR hates meritocracy! An ACTIONATOR will not tolerate being adequate. An ACTIONATOR will persevere until she becomes exceptional! Invite The Actionator to your next event and make ACTIONATORS out of your employees!

Larry Kevin brings with him to every event twenty-five years of experience, inspiring others to take action. His programs are dynamic and entertaining. When Larry Kevin delivers a keynote he has one goal – Make more ACTIONATORS! Do you want to become an ACTIONATOR! **The Actionator** wants to help.

Larry Kevin runs **THE FULL MEASURE,** a consultancy dedicated to ***Engaging People and Organizations in the Pursuit to Fill the Full Measure of Their Creation***. You can find out more about THE FULL MEASURE on the web at www.thefullmeasure.com. Contact information for Larry Kevin can be found at www.larrykevin.com.

Larry Kevin lives with his wife Susan in Indianapolis, Indiana.

Eliot Hoppe is a leading authority on sales mastery, leadership and team development. He is a master at the art of influence, persuasion and non-verbal communication. With over 23 years of sales and leadership experience, Eliot recently completed a successful 11-year tenure with ClearNET Communications and TELUS Corporation, where he spent his entire career in Corporate Sales.

While serving as Director of Sales, Eliot developed the strategy for the national direct sales channel of over 200 account and senior leadership managers. As Director of Recruiting and Training, he was responsible for the national new hire recruitment strategy and the development and implementation of an intensive 3-week sales training program.

Eliot is currently the President of Paramount Learning Systems Inc., which provides leadership coaching and sales training. He is a sought after speaker, coach and corporate sales trainer who has delivered training programs in both Canada and the USA.

He is relentless in his message that the art of selling is a skill that requires constant attention, development and honing. His stories are hilarious and real while his approach is unique, captivating and engaging to all.

Bring Eliot into your organization to deliver quantum results with any of his sales mastery, body language and persuasion programs. Each program is customized to your specific requirements and is guaranteed to compliment any existing corporate sales process.

You can also get more information at www.eliothoppe.com or email him at eliot@eliothoppe.com

Mollie Marti is President of Performance Sciences, Inc., a life and business training and coaching organization.

Performance Sciences offers programs in the areas of human performance, sales, leadership, communication, conflict resolution and personal development. For over ten years, Performance Sciences has partnered with companies, organizations, athletic teams, schools and individuals to establish pathways to excellence and efficiently generate meaningful, long lasting results.
Visit www.performancesciences.net for more information.

Mollie, an Adjunct Assistant Professor of Psychology at the University of Iowa, is widely published in academic journals of psychology and human behavior. As an active researcher and consultant, her knowledge of motivation and performance effectiveness puts her on the cutting edge of performance issues. She provides unique value to corporate clients by motivating their workforce and creating effective selling, marketing, business and leadership strategies to accelerate growth, improve productivity and increase profits.

As a trainer and speaker, Mollie combines a rich personal history of motivating and leading teams to success with a genuine passion for empowering others to live fulfilling and successful lives. She speaks from a place of deep conviction and a lifetime of accomplishments, drawing on years of experience in direct selling, business management, business ownership, law practice, coaching and consulting. She delivers real-world wisdom and scientific research coupled with inspirational stories and humor in a way that moves and motivates audiences to produce lasting results.

Contact Mollie at marti@performancesciences.net or
(319) 361-7691 for additional information on how she can help you and your team take your performance to the next level.

Gary May was born and bred in Southampton, on the south coast of England. From an early age Gary displayed an inquisitive, bright intelligence. He passed his Mathematics GCSE at the age of 14 and pursued studies for the next 12 years in electronics culminating in a degree course in electrical design.

Gary's career has been spent exclusively in the telecommunications and technology sector; as a front line engineer, business owner, product developer, sales consultant, trainer and director of one of the most successful sales teams in the UK telecommunications industry. He has now built a detailed knowledge and understanding of products, solutions and markets.

As a sales manager and trainer Gary has developed a keen, analytical yet creative interest in the psychology of buying and selling. The desire to study and question has quickly made Gary one of the UK's foremost authorities on sales strategy, body language and sub-conscious selling. His fresh ideas quite literally make companies money!

Gary discovered Kevin Hogan on the Internet in 2003, and having devoured all of his material, finally met Kevin in 2006. Gary was invited to become a Platinum Circle Member in that year and a key contributor at Kevin's US seminars in 2007.

Family life is incredibly important to Gary who now lives in the Hampshire countryside with his partner Kat and two sons. Gary can often be found mixing his own mp3 tracks in his spare time, watching his beloved Southampton FC and loves dancing & a glass of good vintage red wine!

Website: www.garymay.co.uk
E-mail: gary@garymay.co.uk

Dave Lakhani is considered one of the nation's top experts on Persuasion and Applied Propaganda. An in demand speaker, Dave trains nearly 100,000 people each year on the topic of applied persuasion from the largest stages in the world. Dave was also The American Business Awards Runner Up for Best Sales Trainer in America in 2007. Dave is considered one of the world's top platform closers who regularly closes 20 – 70% of the people in the rooms he works and is often invited to speak at the largest personal development events in the world and around the world. His understanding of persuasion, behavior and human motivation make him an in demand sales and marketing trainer, and hired gun to close deals.

Dave Lakhani is the President of Bold Approach, Inc., the nation's first Business Acceleration Strategy firm. A business acceleration strategy firm is a company that helps companies seduce consumers, build relationships, dominate top of mind awareness and create powerful personal and company brands . . . *FAST*. Bold Approach was nominated as one of Fast Company Magazine's **Fast 50** companies.

Dave has been responsible for developing dynamic strategies driving record-breaking growth and increases in sales in more than 500 businesses in the past 10 years. Dave is an in demand speaker, author and trainer, whose ideas have been applied by some of the biggest companies in the United States including IBM, US Army, Rogers Media, Micron, GE, Wizard Academy and many more. Dave's advice is frequently seen in magazines including Selling Power, Sales and Marketing Management, Entrepreneur, Business Solutions, and more.

Website: www.boldapproach.com

Kevin Hogan has become the leading resource for analyzing the body language and communication styles of key White House figures. Hogan was consulted on the body language of the Presidential and Vice-Presidential candidates during the 2004 elections. Hogan has taught Persuasion and Influence at the University of St. Thomas Management Center and is a frequent media guest. In 2004 he spoke in Sydney, Australia about what motivates employees from all around the globe. In 2005 he trained some of the world's finest investment bankers in Bologna, Italy and was an invited guest at Maserati International Headquarters. He was recently featured in a half dozen magazines (including wProst) in Poland after teaching persuasion and influence skills to that country's 350 leading sales managers.

His keynotes, seminars and workshops help companies sell, market and communicate more effectively. His cutting-edge research into the mind and keen understanding of consumer behavior create a unique distillation of information never before released to the public. Each customized program he leads is fit specifically to the needs of the group or organization. Kevin will give your people new and easy to implement ideas to achieve excellence.

Coffee with Kevin Hogan, the weekly e-newsletter read by the top sales and marketing people around the world, is available by no-cost subscription at <u>www.kevinhogan.com</u>.

To make Kevin Hogan the dynamic speaker (read that as *very dynamic, funny, informative and knock 'em dead!)* for your next event, go to <u>www.kevinhogan.net.</u>

Need a consultant for your company or firm? Kevin's helped many and might be able to help you too.